BUILDING OUT IN1

In this book, Robert Caper provides the reader with an introduction to psychoanalysis focusing explicitly on whether psychoanalysis is part of the sciences, and if not, where it belongs.

Many psychoanalysts, beginning with Freud, have considered their discipline a science. In this book, Caper examines this claim and investigates the relationship of theory to observation in both philosophy and the experimental sciences and explores how these observations differ from those made in psychoanalytic interpretation. *Building Out into the Dark* also explores topics including:

- the origins of psychoanalysis in the art of medicine
- the therapeutic effect of psychoanalysis
- the archaic superego
- psychoanalysis with the individual and groups
- what makes psychoanalytic work unique.

Building Out into the Dark offers a thoughtful consideration of the nature of psychoanalytic knowledge and how it is gained. The book's accessible and concise style makes it a useful introductory resource for students studying psychoanalysis, for psychotherapists who are curious about the distinction between psychoanalysis and other forms of therapy as well as those interested in placing psychoanalysis in the context of current cultural and intellectual developments.

Robert Caper is Assistant Clinical Professor, University of California at Los Angeles School of Medicine. He is the author of numerous psychoanalytic and scientific research papers and of two books, *Immaterial Facts: Freud's Discovery of Psychic Reality and Klein's Development of His Work* and *A Mind of One's Own*. He has served on the editorial boards of the *Journal of the American Psychoanalytic Association* and the *International Journal of Psychoanalysis*.

BUILDING OUT INTO THE DARK

Theory and observation in science and psychoanalysis

Robert Caper

Routledge
Taylor & Francis Group

LONDON AND NEW YORK

First published 2009
by Routledge
27 Church Road, Hove, East Sussex BN3 2FA

Simultaneously published in the USA and Canada
by Routledge
270 Madison Avenue, New York NY 10016

Routledge is an imprint of the Taylor & Francis Group, an Informa business

Typeset in Times by Garfield Morgan, Swansea, West Glamorgan
Printed and bound in Great Britain by TJ International Ltd, Padstow, Cornwall
Paperback cover design by Gerald Myers

This publication has been produced with paper manufactured to strict
environmental standards and with pulp derived from sustainable forests.

British Library Cataloguing in Publication Data
A catalogue record for this book is available from the British Library

Library of Congress Cataloging in Publication Data
Caper, Robert.
  Building out into the dark : theory and observation in science and
psychoanalysis / Robert Caper.
     p. ; cm.
  Includes bibliographical references and index.
  ISBN 978-0-415-46680-6 (hbk) – ISBN 978-0-415-46681-3 (pbk)
  1. Psychoanalysis. 2. Observation (Scientific method) I. Title.
  [DNLM: 1. Psychoanalytic Theory. WM 460 C239b 2009]
  RC506.C295 2009
  616.89'17–dc22
                                                                2008026169

ISBN: 978–0–415–46680–6 (hbk)
ISBN: 978–0–415–46681–3 (pbk)

It may be that this first portion of our psychological study of dreams will leave us with a sense of dissatisfaction. But we can console ourselves with the thought that we have been obliged to build our way out into the dark.

Freud, *The Interpretation of Dreams*

CONTENTS

CONTENTS

CONTENTS

ACKNOWLEDGMENTS

The author would like to thank Dr. Priscilla Roth and Dr. Michael Paul for their careful review and many valuable suggestions, and Jean Strouse for her extraordinary editorial assistance.

Some parts of Chapter 2 are taken from "The goals of clinical psychoanalysis: Notes on interpretation and psychological development". First published in © The Psychoanalytic Quarterly, 2001, *The Psychoanalytic Quarterly*, 70(1): 99–116, 2001.

Chapter 7 is an expanded version of "Squaring the circle: A review of *Taming Wild Thoughts* by W.R. Bion". First published in *Psychoanalytic Books*, 10(2): 125–133, 1999.

1
INTRODUCTION

1

INTRODUCTION

When we hear the word science, we usually think of something like physics, chemistry, astronomy or geology – "hard" sciences that deal with objects that can be apprehended directly through the five senses. Practitioners of these sciences make observations about the natural world, formulate theories or hypotheses about what they observe, and test competing hypotheses against one another using a regular method that they and their colleagues accept as valid.

Of the boundless variety of things the world presents for observation, relatively few count as scientific evidence. Legitimate evidence in a scientific discipline consists only of observations that scientists may use to support or undermine some scientific hypothesis.

In other words, observations must pass through a screen before they can count as scientific evidence. The screen consists of the very scientific hypotheses and theories that scientists test with their observations: only those observations that fit these hypotheses and theories either positively or negatively – as confirmation or refutation – count as evidence. At the same time, only hypotheses or theories that are subject to confirmation or refutation by this evidence qualify as legitimate.

This apparent circularity does not mean that science, which regularly makes new and unexpected discoveries, is circular. But it does mean that science is circumscribed. In any scientific discipline, only certain types of theories – those that can match up with legitimate evidence – are allowed. At the same time, only certain types of observation – those that match up with

1

legitimate theories – are admitted. (The cosmologist James Jeans summed up this state of affairs by admonishing his students, only half jokingly, never to accept a new observation until it had been thoroughly checked against existing theory.) Theories and observations that do not fit together in this way lie beyond the scope of scientific disciplines.

The "hard" sciences explore phenomena that scientists can apprehend with their physical senses, control for purposes of experimental manipulation and study in numbers large enough to permit rigorous statistical analysis. For example, the question whether Type I, Type II or Type III pneumococcus is the most virulent cause of pneumonia in humans is a legitimate one because scientists can observe pneumococci and their effects through the five senses and can replicate pneumococci at will, thereby providing themselves with vast numbers of identical individuals they can manipulate experimentally. Thanks to these vast numbers, they can analyze the results of such experiments using powerful statistical tools. The observation of large numbers of material objects in controlled experimental settings makes hard science durable, precise and reliable.

One of the things we tend not to think of when we hear the word science is psychoanalysis. At first glance, this seems unremarkable. What could be more different from a scientist working in a laboratory filled with esoteric apparatus than two individuals in a room having a conversation? And psychoanalysis indisputably lacks the elements characteristic of hard science.

In place of objects perceptible to the senses, it studies objects perceptible to sensibility. What we perceive through the senses ("any of the faculties by which stimuli from outside or inside the body are received and felt, as the faculties of hearing, sight, smell, touch, taste, and equilibrium") are material objects. What we perceive through our sensibilities ("mental or emotional responsiveness toward something, such as the feelings of another; refined awareness and appreciation in matters of feeling") are immaterial objects: states of mind, beauty, grace, ugliness, good and evil, values.

Psychoanalysis explores the depths of single, unique human minds. It does not study identical objects in numbers large enough to permit controlled experimentation or statistical analysis of results.

2

Despite these obvious differences, many psychoanalysts, beginning with Freud, have considered their discipline a science. This judgment was certainly less than accurate. It would be tempting to dismiss it as naive if such a dismissal were not itself naive.

The connections and disconnections between science and psychoanalysis are more complex and interesting than the image of the white coated scientist and the tweed coated psychoanalyst would suggest. Both psychoanalysis and science formulate theories or hypotheses; both filter observations through some kind of screen before admitting them as evidence; and both have regular criteria for testing hypotheses against evidence. In psychoanalysis, as in hard science, only certain types of theories – those that can match up with legitimate evidence – are allowed, and only certain types of observation – those that match up with legitimate theories – are admitted. But because of the differences between information that enters through our senses and information that enters through our sensibilities, psychoanalysts must use a fundamentally different kind of "matching" between hypotheses and evidence: in place of controlled experimentation psychoanalysis uses naturalistic observation and in place of statistical analysis, it uses hunch-based reasoning.

Doesn't this settle the matter? Don't the fundamental differences between controlled experimentation and naturalistic observation, on the one hand, and between hunch-based reasoning and statistical analysis, on the other, mean that there is a bright line separating science and psychoanalysis? Yes and no.

It is a commonplace that scientists' theories must be tailored to their observations. It is perhaps less obvious, but no less true, that scientists' methods must be tailored to fit what they are observing. There is no point in studying embryos with an atom-smasher, or atoms with a Petri dish. The methods that scientists employ can never merely be those that work in other fields of study, but must be those dictated by the nature of the matter they are trying to study.

Theory, method and observation are related to each other in complex ways. Theories about the nature of a problem sculpt the method with which one approaches it. One's methods determine at least in part what one will end up observing, and one's observations then modify one's theories. When the relationships between method, theory and observation are sound, theory and method will operate in the service of obtaining new observations. Science develops by enlarging its capacity to observe through developing methods that allow scientists to see things they were previously unable to see.

Psychoanalysis will never be an experimental science. But it is an attempt to develop methods of observation that allow us to see things we could not otherwise see. In this sense, it carries out the spirit of experimental science, even if it cannot follow its letter.

But what does it mean exactly to say that psychoanalysis carries out the spirit of science? And if it doesn't follow the letter of science, what letter does it follow? When we look at it carefully, do we have reason to believe that the psychoanalytic method is any more than unscientific speculation about unknowable quantities? These are some of the questions I will address in this book.

2

PSYCHOANALYSIS AND SCIENCE

If we compare theory formation in psychoanalysis with theory formation in the experimental sciences, we find that in the experimental sciences, theories are established when hypotheses are subjected to the test of controlled experiment.[1] Controlled experimentation is the *sine qua non* of experimental science, and an hypothesis becomes a well-established theory in the experimental sciences only by being subjected to its rigors.

Once established, theories in the experimental sciences may be used to replace actual experience in future specific instances of the phenomena to which the theories apply. For example, Bernoulli's Principle, which began as an hypothesis about the relationship between the movement of a fluid and the pressure it exerts on adjacent surfaces, has been so fully verified by controlled experiment that aeronautical engineers now use it to predict very precisely how much lift a certain wing design will produce. Aircraft designers need not, therefore, construct a series of wings and test them by trial and error in order to know how to build a wing with the desired amount of lift. They may instead use Bernoulli's Principle to calculate the lift that a given design will produce.

Psychoanalysis resembles the experimental sciences in that it forms hypotheses that are tested against evidence on their way to becoming established (or not) as theories. But while theories

---

1 Parts of this chapter are taken from "The goals of clinical psychoanalysis: Notes on interpretation and psychological development" [14].

in the experimental sciences are established by the construction of controlled experiments, psychoanalytic theories are established by the absorption of the uncontrolled experience of the psychoanalytic session.

This fundamental difference in how theories are established reflects differences in the subject matters psychoanalysis and science address. Theories in the experimental sciences may be validated by means of controlled experiment because in experimental science the phenomena being studied are replicable. In other words, these phenomena may be set up in parallel groups, where each group contains large (statistically significant) numbers of more or less identical individuals, and where the members of one group differ from those of the other by only one relevant variable.[2] The fact of replicability in the physical sciences makes possible the controlled experimentation and statistical analysis that allows theories to be established with a high degree of precision and certainty.

Psychoanalysis studies phenomena that cannot be replicated or controlled in any precise way. This difficulty is not simply due to the complexity of mental phenomena. The problem lies at a more fundamental level: the events that psychoanalysis studies are states of mind, which are not replicable. They are never precisely the same from one moment to the next, and no two individuals can be said to have states of mind that are "the same" enough to permit the kind of controlled experimentation that would win the respect of experimental scientists. Even more significantly, the variables that are relevant to states of mind cannot be controlled and manipulated for experimental purposes.

Because psychoanalytic theories cannot be confirmed by controlled experiment, they cannot be used to replace direct experience in specific cases the way the theories of the experimental

---

2 Strictly speaking, these two groups differ by only one known relevant variable. There may be other relevant variables that are unknown, but the use of large numbers of individuals in each group makes it statistically likely that these other variables, even though unknown, will be distributed evenly between the two groups and thus cancel each other out. The larger the numbers in the groups, the more likely the variables are to be evenly distributed and the more reliable the result. Hence the importance of large numbers in experimental science.

sciences, such as Bernoulli's Principle, can. On the contrary, to the degree that analysts try to emulate engineers by attempting to use psychoanalytic theory in place of direct trial and error experience with their patients, they fall short of analyzing their patients.

Psychoanalysts commonly recognize in the patient's material an instance of some general theory or piece of knowledge the analyst already has – "this is splitting" (or Oedipal conflict, or denial, or reaction formation). But analysts who fail to move themselves (or be moved by their experience in the analysis) beyond what was already encompassed by their theories before their encounter with the patient are courting analytic sterility.[3] Analysts cannot simply assume that the clinical problem at hand represents a specific instance of a general law, and then apply the general law to the specific instance, since the loss of specific, idiosyncratic detail that such generalizing would entail would have a disastrous effect on the realism of the resulting interpretation. On the contrary, analysts can arrive at an effective theory – a good interpretation – only by carefully absorbing as much as they can of the detail that is unique and specific to their clinical experience with one patient.

For this reason, analysts must maintain a state of highly polished ignorance about what the patient presents them with, until their experience of the patient impresses something on them. An aeronautical engineer who tried to design an airplane in this fashion would be a very bad engineer, having to reinvent the Wright Flyer each time; but an analyst who did not proceed in this manner would be a very bad analyst. Psychoanalysts, for practical purposes, must reinvent the wing each time they make an interpretation.

These differences between psychoanalysis and the experimental sciences may be summarized as follows:

A Experimental science deals with large classes of individuals, that is, individuals who are more or less indistinguishable,

---

3 In John Rickman's words, "no research without therapy, no therapy without research" [32, p. 213].

or whose differences can be washed out in statistical analysis without destroying what made them interesting to study in the first place.

Psychoanalysis does not deal with large classes of individuals, but with single individuals whose differences may not be washed out without major loss of significance.

B   Dealing with large classes of individuals permits scientists to produce a body of theory with highly specific predictive value that can, to a considerable degree, eliminate the need for direct and detailed investigation of individual cases.

Dealing with single individuals does not permit psychoanalysts to make theoretical generalizations of the type that may be substituted for direct experience.

C   Experimental science conducts its investigations by relying on an established body of experimentally derived theoretical knowledge.

Psychoanalysis does not rely for its investigations on an established body of theoretical knowledge, but investigates unique cases using a technique of creative exploration.

D   Expertise in experimental science is associated with knowledge of a body of theory.

Expertise in psychoanalysis consists of the capacity to work in ignorance of theory – to see what one is looking at without theoretical preconceptions.

Ignoring the differences between (non-replicable) mental and (replicable) physical phenomena, and the differences in methodology required for the study of each, poses the gravest risk to anyone interested in understanding the mind. In his book *Learning from Experience* (1962) [4], the psychoanalyst Wilfred Bion writes of a patient whose thought processes lacked the qualities of depth, resonance and evocativeness that one associates with the human mind, and seemed to be the product not of a mind, but of a machine. From the data of the patient's analysis, he draws a picture of the mental "organ" whose impairment resulted in this state of affairs, and reconstructs what might have happened to this patient. This reconstruction is worth recounting in some detail.

Bion begins by taking seriously the common-sense notion that, just as infants need physical care and comfort, they also need love,[4] from which it follows that, under normal circumstances, an infant must have the capacity to perceive love – a kind of "sense organ" for love – much as it has sense organs for perceiving other vital necessities such as food and warmth. To perceive the love it needs, the infant must be able to bear the emotional strain of realizing that its well-being and even its survival depends on something as uncontrollable as its mother's love. Bion considers the extreme case of an infant completely unable to bear this strain. Such an infant might blind itself to these unbearable needs and to the love, solace and understanding that would both elicit and satisfy them.[5]

An infant who destroys its "sense organ" for love in this way grows into an adult like one of Bion's patients, who greedily pursued every form of material comfort in a vain effort to supply himself with the non-material comfort he lacked but could not even recognize. Such an infant eventually comes to live in a perceptual world composed only of material objects, and inevitably becomes like a material object himself, with machine-like thought processes. To Bion, this mental mechanization represents a breakdown in the patient's equipment for thinking about emotional realities that leaves the patient living in a universe populated by emotionless objects that Bion calls "inanimate."

He then moves beyond the immediate clinical problem to reflect on its wider scientific significance: the scientific methods and modes of thought that are appropriate to an understanding of the inanimate world (such as those of physics or chemistry), or to an understanding of the mechanical aspects of biological or social systems (such as those of physiology and behaviorism),

---

4 The truth of this commonplace has been driven home by Schlossman's [35] classic observations of "hospitalism": the dramatic and unaccountably high mortality rate among unwanted infants housed on large orphanage wards whose physical needs were seen to with great efficiency by a staff too busy to make emotional contact with them.

5 We consider such extreme cases not because they are the rule, or even common, but because their extremity throws into sharp relief the matter we wish to consider. There is no question that infants vary widely in their capacity to tolerate the type of strain we are positing. Why this is so is widely and hotly debated in psychoanalysis.

yield models that are mechanical and therefore inappropriate for understanding the mind.

When we see a patient such as Bion's treating mental events as though they were subject to manipulation and control like the stuff of physics and engineering, we say the patient suffers from the type of thought disorder known as concrete thinking. This diagnostic label obscures the fact that the difference between such a patient's approach to the mind and the scientist's is only a matter of degree. It is very difficult for anyone entirely to escape concrete thinking when trying to form firm, precise, predictive conclusions about the human mind. Psychoanalysis is, among other things, a battle against this kind of concrete thinking. It brings about psychological development not just by discovering new information, but by bringing about a change in patients' perspectives or attitudes toward their own mind – a new relationship to their mind. After a successful analysis, patients are more able to treat the events occurring in their mind as mental.

The wish to treat states of mind as though they were inanimate objects – to predict, control and manipulate them, or to get rid of unwanted pieces of them, or to transform their nature at will – is common even among patients without manifest thought disorders, many of whom secretly hope to achieve precisely this kind of control from psychoanalysis. A successful analysis not only fails to fulfill this dream of control, but also confirms what from the patient's point of view might seem like a nightmare – a mind out of control, which many patients equate with madness. It is the analyst's task to show the patient that going "mad" in this way may actually be sane, and that clinging to the controlled sanity the patient hopes for may actually be mad.

For analysts to be able to help the patient achieve this perspective on the contents of his mind, they must have it well installed in their own. They must recognize that events taking place in the mind – theirs and the patient's – are autonomous. They appear as if of their own volition, and all the analyst can do is observe their appearance and try to ponder what they are and how they might be connected to other events. This attitude acknowledges the sovereignty of mental events: the mind is subject to mental events, but mental events cannot be subjugated by the mind.[6] Although psychoanalysts discover this fundamental principle again and again clinically, and although what is perhaps the most basic psychoanalytic theory – the theory of the unconscious – acknowledges this principle, very often psychoanalytic practice proceeds as though the sovereignty of the mind can be ignored, as, for example, when analysts lapse into making "interpretations" that are intended to control or change the patient's mind, instead of being intended merely to inform the patient while leaving him completely free in his use of the information provided.

Freud's most important achievement was not a series of empirical discoveries about how the mind works (repression, the Oedipus complex, etc.), but reaching an attitude toward mental events that recognizes their fundamental autonomy and uncontrollability. Recognizing the sovereign nature of mental events reduces the analyst and patient to the status of observers, describers and ponderers of states of mind that emerge of their own accord in the course of an analysis.

But of course, the situation is considerably more complicated than that. The word "observers" fails to convey the almost complete immersion of both working patient and working analyst in the emotional events they are trying to describe and assess. Mental events of the type psychoanalysis is concerned with not only cannot be controlled in the way physical events can be, but also cannot even be observed in the dispassionate way physical events may be. They can only be lived through.

Psychoanalytic technique: building out into the dark

Psychoanalytic technique consists of analysts allowing the patient's unconscious to have an impact on their own unconscious, and observing the conscious emotional experiences that develop as a result. Analysts then use these experiences to build their way out into the dark of the immediate, live interaction between themselves and the patient, and from there back into the patient's unconscious. To accomplish this, analysts must be

6 This is related to Bion's idea of "thoughts without a thinker": thoughts are not produced by the mind, but the mind instead forms to deal with the "thoughts" – spontaneous mental events – with which it is presented.

able to tolerate being in the dark. Too much light (too little dark) is a sign that a tendency toward omniscience may have replaced learning from experience in the analyst's mind. A carefully preserved ignorance and naivety are essential to the practice of a therapeutic analysis, since they defend analysts' capacity to learn against their psychoanalytic omniscience, i.e. what they may falsely feel they know in a general or theoretical way. Psychoanalytic expertise (in any practically useful sense of the term) does not consist of a body of knowledge, but of knowing how to remain ignorant long enough to have new experiences of a patient from which one may learn.

Psychoanalysis depends on surprise – on the discovery of what was not previously known, perhaps not even suspected. Such discovery depends on analysts' capacity to preserve the mystery of a novel experience long enough to contemplate it and to be surprised by what they have found. The rescue of mystery and surprise from the "knowledge" that destroys them is another way of formulating the goal of clinical psychoanalysis.

But mystery, once restored, tends always to be once more eroded away. What has newly been learned comes quickly to be "known" in a way that allows it to act as a defense against further mysteries, surprises and learning. The capacity to be mystified must therefore be regained over and over in an analysis. This dialectic of emergence from false knowledge (omniscience) into mystery, then falling back again, and emerging again, over and over, is the dialectic of psychoanalytic development.[7]

The replacement of omniscience by a sense of mystery in an analysis – the restoration of healthy ignorance – means recognizing that we cannot know or control other people's unconscious minds any more than we can know or control our own. This recognition is a sign of respect for the essential separateness of other people from oneself. If analysts feel that they have learned something about their patient that does not immediately present them with further mysteries, they are likely to be engaging

---

7 This is the dialectic between the paranoid-schizoid and depressive positions, summarized by Bion's formulation PS↔D, if we interpret PS (which is similar to Klein's paranoid-schizoid position) as a state of certainty and security and D (similar to Klein's depressive position) as a state of doubt and insecurity (i.e., in a manner opposite to that in which they are often interpreted).

in a defense against the anxiety that the essential separateness and uncontrollability of the patient's mind arouses in the analyst.

What assurance we have that an interpretation is likely to be valid, given that interpretations more closely resemble the products of the artist's intuition response to the materials than scientific hypotheses that can be verified by controlled experimentation? How do we know that an interpretation is not simply an artistic creation – an aesthetically competent but otherwise arbitrary communication? When making a valid interpretation, analysts have worked through the emotional impact on themselves of what the patient is conveying to the point that they are able to observe it in a disinterested way. This state of mind is marked by a sense of mystery, an awareness of a lack of control over mental events, and a sense that the patient is mentally separate from the analyst. The observations made in an analysis while the analyst is in this state of mind may be taken as (relatively) valid in the same way that the images produced by an astronomical telescope whose optics are known to be in (relatively) good order may be taken as valid.

Another sign that the analyst's mind is working well as an analytic instrument is analysts' ability to perceive the patient through the veil of their own preconceptions, to discover the aspects of the experience they are living through with the patient that were not encompassed by their theories. A third sign is analysts' ability to refrain from using what they discover for any purpose other than conveying information to the patient. This means that analysts must listen without omniscience (the need to have theoretical preconceptions about the patient, or to "know") or desire (the need to fix or reassure the patient, as opposed to merely conveying information to the patient about himself).[8]

---

8 I am aware that these criteria for the validity of a psychoanalytic interpretation refer entirely to the analyst's subjective state, and are unlikely to convince skeptics because they lack the safeguard built into the practice of experimental science: the replication of controlled observations by independent researchers. I cannot help this, but I can point out that careful and disinterested observation – free of preconceptions and wishful thinking – as I am describing it is precisely what enables experimental scientists to make observations that stand the test of replication. Their observations are valid because they are well and carefully made;

Omniscience and desire are constantly being stimulated in the working analyst. Much of the work of analysis consists of self-analysis of the omniscience and desires that the analysis does stimulate in the analyst (and that form part of the analyst's unconscious countertransference). The product of this analysis is an interpretation that, to the degree that the self-analysis was successful, will be spoken solely to convey information to the patient, not as an attempt to control, cure or otherwise reduce the patient to the status of the inanimate.[9]

The importance of an interpretation not being an attempt to cure the patient becomes clearer if we consider that "curing the patient" is usually an attempt to kill something in the patient's mind, or to trim the patient's mind to fit the analyst's preconception of what the patient is or should be like, rather than to do what analysis can do uniquely well: improve the patient's capacity to be in contact with and to tolerate his mind as it is, so that patients may develop on their own. In addition, working analysts must live through an emotional experience with their patient, then think about this experience in a disinterested way, and then convey what they have gleaned from this to the patient in a way that is free from suggestion, coercion or any hint that it is anything other than how things are *in the analyst's opinion.*

Or rather, analysts must try to do this. One of the paradoxes of analysis, as I have indicated, is that the analytic situation could hardly be better calculated to make it impossible for analysts to maintain this objective, non-tendentious stance. It is precisely this impossibility that makes the analysis alive, and also provides analysts with one of the most important sources of new knowledge about their patient. The ways in which analysts get pulled out of the position of listening without preconceptions and of speaking only to convey information to the patient, allows them to be in contact with the immediate experience that

---

replication only confirms what was true even before the results were replicated. A psychoanalytic interpretation made in the way I am describing may be quite valid despite the impossibility of demonstrating this to anyone not involved in the analysis. For a fuller discussion of some of these points, see "What is a clinical fact?" [11].

9 This is a complex point that I explore at greater length in "Does psychoanalysis heal?" [10].

they and their patient are living through, which gives analysts vital information about what they need to describe to the patient. Analysts need to have a great deal of the experience of being pulled out of their analytic attitude by emotional forces originating in themselves and/or their patient, and of being able to regain that attitude, before they can have the courage and conviction necessary to allow themselves to be pulled out of it and still feel they will be able regularly to return later.

To summarize this point: the criteria I am proposing for ascertaining the validity of an interpretation in the absence of the possibility of controlled experimentation is that it be arrived at while analysts are in a state of mind in which they are not attempting to control or modify the object (their own or another's mind) and that preserves a healthy ignorance about the matter at hand.[10] Preservation of ignorance is not the same as simply being ignorant or mystified. It is a type of knowledge: the knowledge that one is in the presence of something unknown. However, the analytic relationship could not be better calculated to stir up in the analyst anxieties and desires about the person they are in the analytic relationship with, and thereby to create the need to control them. A psychoanalytically productive state of mind can be achieved only through experiencing and working through this need. To the degree this working through has been done, the resulting analytic perspective is likely to be one that yields valid interpretations. In all of this, I am making the assumption that we can see the truth if nothing is pulling us away from it, and that the ways in which we find ourselves getting pulled away from it are an important part of the truth we need to see in an analysis.

The goals of clinical psychoanalysis

W.R. Bion, in his book *Transformations*, suggests that the product of the analyst's work may be considered either

---

10 I refer here to the "analyst's" state of mind, but I am of course aware that the patient may be in this state of mind as well – sometimes even more than the analyst. In this case, the patient will be working better analytically than the analyst. Since it doesn't matter who moves the analysis along, what I am saying can apply to either party in the analysis.

the analyst's verbalization of his experience in the session, or the emotional state induced in his patient . . . *Since psycho-analysts do not aim to run the patient's life but to enable him to run it according to his lights and therefore to know what his lights are, [the analyst's communications] either in the form of interpretation or scientific paper should represent [only] the psychoanalyst's verbal representation of an emotional experience . . . [the analyst's communication] must be limited so that it expresses truth without any implication other than the implication that it is true in the analyst's opinion.* How is truth to be a criterion [for an interpretation]? To what has it to be true and how shall we decide whether it is or not . . . Falling back on analytic experience for a clue . . . in practice the problem arises with . . . personalities in whom the superego appears to be developmentally prior to the ego and to deny development and existence itself to the ego. The usurpation by the superego of the position that should be occupied by the ego involves imperfect development of the reality principle, exaltation of a "moral" outlook and lack of respect for the truth. The result is starvation of the psyche and stunted growth. I shall regard this statement as an axiom that resolves more difficulties than it creates.

[6, pp. 37–8, emphasis mine]

The product of the analyst's work is psychoanalytic (rather than propagandistic) only if analysts verbalize nothing but their own emotional experience of their patient, and only then if they can do so in a way that conveys that what they are saying is only their take on the emotional events occurring in the consulting room. The patient is left free to choose how to use the analyst's communication. The analyst should add to the patient's experience, but the type of experience the analyst adds to the patient's life should be one that only informs the patient of something, leaving patients free to think for themselves and moreover to run their lives according to their own lights. The alternative to this approach is a moralistic one, what Bion called "usurpation by the superego of the position that should be occupied by the ego", in which the analyst disregards the truth in favor of inducing an emotional state in the patient (positive or negative) that acts to control the patient.

In other words, analysts can promote growth in their patient (and avoid controlling him) only by keeping constantly in their (and their patient's) view that what they say is true *only in their opinion*. This healthy modesty has two consequences. First, it undermines the patient's belief that the analysis will solve his problems, and second, it leaves patients free to solve their own problems, that is, to live their own lives. Only in this way does the analyst leave the patient free to choose how to use the product of the analyst's work, and only in this way can the analyst avoid being what Bion calls a superego that usurps the patient's rights.

The analyst's awareness of the limitations of his knowledge is crucially important because the analyst's clinical work, whatever scientific or artistic validity it might have, is fundamentally an ethical activity: the broadening of patients' experience, and especially their experience of themselves, in a way that leaves them free to use that experience as they see fit.

I have described four perspectives on the goal of clinical psychoanalysis:

- to increase patients' capacity to experience their mental life as mental, meaning not subject to their control, manipulation or precise prediction
- to increase patients' capacity to feel, and to think about what they feel
- to rescue patients' capacity for surprise, and for seeing new things as new, from the kind of false knowledge that obstructs new experience
- to broaden patients' experience of themselves in a way that sets them free to use this broadened experience to live their own lives.

I call these four perspectives on a single goal of clinical psychoanalysis, rather than four goals, because they are different aspects of the same thing. A capacity to acknowledge the autonomy of one's mental life is clearly related to the capacity to feel what actually is in one's mind (as opposed to what one wishes to be

17

there), and to the capacity to experience how one actually is, despite how one feels one is supposed to be.

While these are four perspectives on the same thing, they only point toward, rather than define, precisely what that thing is. But perhaps as a practical guide to the goal of clinical psychoanalysis, it is worth recalling Charcot's words: *"La theorie c'est bon, mais ce n'empêche pas d'exister"* (Theories are good, but they don't preclude things from being what they are) [17, p. 13].

3

PSYCHOANALYSIS AND SCIENCE
Rules and games

Sciences are characterized by certain fundamental premises – notions without which a given scientific discipline would not exist. For example, the notions of space, time and mass are fundamental premises of physics. It is difficult to imagine what physics would look like if any of those notions were discarded. Similarly, the notion of natural selection is a fundamental premise in evolutionary biology: it is difficult to imagine any theory in modern evolutionary biology that does not depend, directly or indirectly, on the validity of the notion of natural selection.

One may always reject these premises, but without them it would be difficult to do physics or evolutionary biology in any recognizable form. These fundamental premises are like rules of a game. One may accept them or not, but one cannot both reject them and still play the game (although one may, of course, reject them and play another game, with different rules). In this sense, these fundamental notions define a certain game, a certain discipline, and all who accept them are playing the same game, however much their activities within the game may differ.

In sciences such as physics, biology and medicine, these fundamental premises – the "rules of the game" – may be combined with new observations to produce theories. A physicist could ask, "Given the ideas of space, time, force and mass, what happens when we exert force on masses in space over time?" Observations intended to answer this question have pointed to certain regularities that are embodied in Newton's laws of motion. Theories such as these are subsidiary to the

19

fundamental premises in a field in the sense that they may turn out to be true or false (or only partly true, as, for example, Einstein's revision shows Newton's laws of motion to be). But even if subsidiary theories are shown to be false, the fundamental premises remain valid. They remain so because the premises that are fundamental to a discipline are not subject to validation, confirmation or disconfirmation within a field; if one rejects them, one has simply left the field, and is playing a different game. Fundamental premises define a certain discipline, while the specific theories that might flow from observations made using these fundamental premises as a framework are contingent and dispensable.

Once formulated, specific scientific theories are subject to further challenge and experimental verification. Theories that have been verified many times in many different ways come to be regarded as well established. A well-established theory achieves the status of a fact within the scientific discipline, and may then be combined with new observations to generate new theories.

The fundamental notions of space, force, time and mass in physics, when combined with experimental observation, yields Newton's laws of motion, which have been tested and confirmed so many times in so many different ways that they are now regarded as a kind of fact. The fundamental notion of natural selection in Darwin's theory of evolution, when combined with observation, gives rise to specific theories that are typically and characteristically part of evolutionary theory. (For example, the theory that selective pressures tend to convert geographically isolated populations of the same species into different species.) These theories in turn give rise to predictions that can then be tested against observation.

Like experimental sciences, psychoanalysis has a set of premises that are shared by all psychoanalysts – ideas that seem to be basic rules of the psychoanalytic game. Among them are the notions of an unconscious and of psychological defense mechanisms (which are by definition unconscious). It would be difficult to imagine how a psychoanalyst would function if he did not accept these notions.

But while psychoanalysts, like experimental scientists, have a set of fundamental defining premises, unlike experimental scientists they have not been able to combine their fundamental notions with new observations to give rise to theories that they have tested and universally accepted. Psychoanalysts have certainly generated theories and tested them against their clinical experience. But despite the fact that they all share fundamental assumptions that define psychoanalysis as a discipline, and are all in a position to make the same kinds of observations, they have not been able to combine these fundamental premises with observations to generate theories that, like those of physics or evolutionary biology, have become part of a theoretical canon.

Consider the germ theory of disease, which holds that certain illnesses are caused by microorganisms, that these diseases may be transmitted from one person to another by physical transfer of these organisms, and that the disease in question cannot occur in the absence of these organisms. This theory is not one of the fundamental premises of medicine, since we could imagine medicine without it (as it was before the mid-nineteenth century – very different from modern medicine, but still recognizably medicine). But it has been tested in so many varied situations that its validity is universally accepted by physicians. It is a well-established theory.

With this in mind, consider any psychoanalytic theory, such as the theory of the Oedipus complex. Today, even this theory is not accepted by some analysts who still subscribe wholeheartedly to the fundamental premises of psychoanalysis. For them, Oedipal phenomena are contingent, arising only as a consequence of certain less-than-optimal childhood environments. Other analysts cannot imagine thinking psychoanalytically without this theory. For them, it is part of the foundation of their psychoanalytic picture of the mind, and they cannot picture psychoanalysis without it. In neither case is it a well-established theory in the same way that the germ theory of disease is in medicine: for one group it is a theory but not well established, and for the other it is well established, but not a theory (since it is for them a fundamental premise – an indispensable part of their picture of psychoanalysis).

Or take the theory of projective identification in psychoanalysis. There are many analysts who regard it as having questionable validity, and as not very useful in any event. There are others who would be hard pressed to practice analysis

21

without it. I don't mean they would find it difficult to treat only certain patients, the way a physician would if he didn't have the germ theory. I mean they would be hard pressed to treat any patient without it. The former type of analyst regards projective identification as a more or less dispensable idea, while the latter finds it a fundamental part of their psychoanalytic concept of how the mind works, indispensable in all cases.

I could add to these examples. But the point I am trying to make is that notions in psychoanalysis that are universally accepted tend to fall into the category of fundamental premises – ideas without which practicing the discipline would be hard to imagine. Ideas that do not fall into this category tend not to be universally accepted. This is what I meant when I wrote above that psychoanalysts have not been able to generate subsidiary theories that, like those of physics or evolutionary biology, have won universal acceptance among workers in the field. In psychoanalysis, the only notions that are well established and universally accepted are fundamental premises.[1]

In clinical disciplines, fundamental premises define a general approach to the patient. The psychoanalytic notion of the unconscious, like the Hippocratic notion that physical diseases have natural causes, points to a general approach to the patient, a certain way of listening to, observing and thinking about patients. The idea of the unconscious *defines* the psychoanalytic approach to the patient, and distinguishes it from the religious, magical or medical approaches, as well as from the approach taken by non-psychoanalytic psychologies. The unconscious is a rule of the psychoanalytic game: an idea that is not discovered or established by evidence or argument, but is simply adopted as a fundamental premise or definition. In fact, it is *the* rule of the psychoanalytic game. If a physician were to reject the idea that diseases have natural (as opposed to supernatural) causes, he would no longer be practicing medicine. If a psychoanalyst

---

1 As the above examples have indicated, although certain fundamental premises, such as the notion of the unconscious and of defense mechanisms, are shared by all analysts, different groups of analysts share additional fundamental premises. What this means for the status of psychoanalysis as a unitary discipline is an interesting question that I cannot go into now, except to say that it may have something to do with the tendency of psychoanalytic groups to fragment.

rejected the idea the unconscious, he would no longer be practicing psychoanalysis. But it is hard to imagine any other notion whose rejection would disqualify him as a psychoanalyst.

This all suggests that psychoanalysis does not have the structure of an experimental science like physics or biology, and not even of an experimental clinical science like endocrinology or the study of infectious diseases. It does have certain fundamental notions that do not need proof or demonstration, but these notions do not combine with observation to give rise to a theoretical canon. Instead they act as tools or instruments that permit certain kinds of observation to be made, and certain things to be looked at in a certain way. To put this in another way, psychoanalysis does not have fundamental premises on which a scientific theoretical system may be built. Rather, it has what might be called a set of conceptual tools, ideas that represent a certain way of looking at things, and that act as instruments with which one may observe things that are otherwise unobservable.

This conclusion is in line with Wittgenstein's when he wrote that Freud's propositions are not the result of discoveries and are not scientific in character, but are simply

something which people are inclined to accept and which makes it easier for them to go certain ways: it makes certain ways of behaving and thinking natural for them. They have given up one way of thinking and adopted another.

[1, pp. 44–5]

In a related passage, Wittgenstein wrote:

One thinks of certain results of psychoanalysis as a discovery Freud made, as apart from something you are persuaded of by a psychoanalyst, and I wish to say this is not the case. Those sentences have the form of persuasion, in particular [those] which say "This is *really* this" [which only means] there are certain differences which you have been persuaded to neglect.

[1, p. 27, original emphasis]

23

If this sounds damning, consider that it comes from a philosopher who considered philosophical problems to be a symptom
of helpless confusion, the philosopher a therapist whose job it is
to "help show the fly the way out of the fly-bottle" by per-
suading him that he's going about it all wrong, and himself (at
least in this specific sense) a disciple of Freud:

> If someone says, "There is not a difference," and I say:
> "There is a difference" I am persuading. I am saying "I
> don't want you to look at it like that" . . . I am in a
> sense making propaganda for one style of thinking as
> opposed to another. I am honestly disgusted with the
> other. Also I'm trying to say what I think. Nevertheless,
> I'm saying: "For God's sake don't do this".

[1, pp. 27–8]

Science and psychoanalysis

In his book *The Scientist as Rebel* [14], the physicist Freeman
Dyson touched on the issue of what I have called the rules of
the game when he observed that:

> there are two extreme points of view concerning the role
> of science in human understanding. At one extreme is
> the reductionist view, holding that all kinds of knowl-
> edge, from physics and chemistry to psychology and
> philosophy and sociology and history and ethics and
> religion, can be reduced to science.

[15, p. 330]

Dyson uses the word "science" in this passage in a narrow sense
– what I have called science by controlled experiment. Extreme
reductionism holds that whatever cannot be verified by science
in this narrow sense is not knowledge. He goes on:

> At the other extreme is the traditional view, that
> knowledge comes from many independent sources, and
> science is only one of them. Knowledge of good and
> evil, knowledge of grace and beauty, knowledge of
> ethical and artistic values, knowledge of human nature

24

derived from history and literature or from intimate acquaintance with family and friends, knowledge of the nature of things derived from meditation or from religion, are all sources of knowledge that stand side by side with science, parts of a human heritage that is older than science and perhaps more enduring. Most people hold views intermediate between the two extremes.

[15, p. 330]

Dyson then goes on to discuss the practical differences between these two views by referring to the problem of paranormal phenomena, a highly controversial subject that is perfectly suited to illustrate what he calls "the question of the proper limits of science":

I agree [with those who say] that attempts to study extrasensory perception and telepathy using the methods of science have failed. [Reductionists] say that since extrasensory perception and telepathy cannot be studied scientifically, they do not exist. Their conclusion is clear and logical, but I do not accept it because I am not a reductionist. I claim that paranormal phenomena may really exist but may not be susceptible to scientific investigation. This is a hypothesis. I am not saying that it is true, only that it is tenable, and to my mind plausible.

The hypothesis that paranormal phenomena are real but lie outside the limits of science is supported by a great mass of evidence. The evidence has been collected by the Society for Psychical Research in Britain and by similar organizations in other countries. The journal of the London Society is full of stories of remarkable events in which ordinary people appear to possess paranormal abilities. The evidence is entirely anecdotal. It has nothing to do with science, since it cannot be reproduced under controlled conditions. But the evidence is there. The members of the society took great trouble to interview firsthand witnesses as soon as possible after the events, and to document the stories carefully. One fact that emerges clearly from the stories is that paranormal events occur, if they occur at all, only when people are under stress and experiencing strong emotion. This fact would immediately explain why paranormal phenomena are not observable under the conditions of a well-controlled scientific experiment. Strong emotion and stress are inherently incompatible with controlled scientific procedures. In a typical card-guessing experiment, the participants may begin the session in a high state of excitement and record a few high scores, but as the hours pass, and boredom replaces excitement, the scores decline to the 20 percent expected from random chance.

[15, pp. 330–1]

Dyson then comes to the point he wishes to make:

I am suggesting that paranormal mental abilities and scientific method [i.e., the method of controlled experimentation] may be complementary. The word "complementary" is a technical terms introduced into physics by Niels Bohr. It means that two descriptions of nature may both be valid but cannot be observed simultaneously. The classic example of complementarity is the dual nature of light. In one experiment light is seen to behave as a continuous wave, in another experiment it behaves like a swarm of particles, but we cannot see the wave and the particles in the same experiment. Complementarity in physics is an established fact. The extension of the idea of complementarity to mental phenomena is pure speculation. But I find it plausible that a world of mental phenomena should exist, too fluid and evanescent to be grasped with the cumbersome tools of science.

[15, p. 331]

Psychoanalysis is another example of a discipline that is complementary with what Dyson calls reductionistic science – science employing the method of controlled experimentation. This type of science has little to say about the areas of human experience encompassed by the terms good and evil, grace and beauty, and ethical and artistic values because these areas do

26

not readily lend themselves to study by controlled experimentation. Until relatively recently, they have been the purview of ethics, aesthetics and other branches of philosophy, where they have been treated systematically and generally, or of literature and history, where they have been treated unsystematically and generally, or of what Dyson called "intimate acquaintance with family and friends", where they have been treated unsystematically and specifically.

Psychoanalysis differs from reductionistic science in the same way as these other disciplines, but it is also unique among them because it deals with these aspects of experience both systematically and specifically, that is, by a regular method that addresses the meaning of these terms within the life of a specific individual. Psychoanalysis is a unique source of knowledge, different from both science in the narrow sense and from literature, philosophy, history and ordinary intimate experience.

4

THE ORIGINS OF PSYCHOANALYSIS IN THE ART OF MEDICINE

The art and science of medicine

In 1905, Freud published an article in which he defined the new therapeutic approach he called "psychical treatment":

> "Psyche" is a Greek word which may be translated "mind". Thus, "psychical treatment" means "mental treatment". The term might accordingly be supposed to signify "treatment of the pathological phenomena of mental life." This, however, is not its meaning. "Psychical treatment" denotes, rather, treatment taking its start in the mind, treatment (whether of mental or physical disorders) by measures which operate in the first instance and immediately upon the human mind.
>
> [18, p. 283]

Although the idea of treating physical disorders with psychological measures sounds to us suspiciously like faith healing, it has a long and honorable lineage. From the time of Hippocrates until only a few hundred years ago, physicians made little distinction between mental and physical factors in therapy. Freud's notion of mental treatment sounds strange because it is in line with the ancient tradition, which ignores the distinction, so ingrained in us now, between the mental and physical treatment of disease.

With the rise of scientific medicine, physicians began to distinguish more incisively between physical and non-physical causes and treatment of disease. Having done this, they directed their attention to the physical aspects of disease, which, as we know, yielded to the scientific approach as though it were made for them.

Research in biochemistry, genetics and human and animal anatomy and physiology has produced models of human disease that not only are suited to systematic scientific investigation, but also suggest rational medical treatments as well. After formulating these treatments, the medical scientist can then validate them in controlled clinical studies, involving large numbers of patients, to establish their efficacy and safety. (Such studies are epitomized by modern trials of new antibiotics, anti-cancer drugs, antidepressants and new surgical procedures.)

Over the past two hundred years, physical medicine has transformed itself from an unsystematic collection of practices based on anecdotal and untested knowledge into a system of practices based on experimentally verifiable theories that, when applied to the treatment of patients, produce results that are also precisely measurable and verifiable.

Being scientifically trained pragmatists, physicians prefer treatments that are scientific and specific to treatments that are unscientific and non-specific. When scientific physical treatment is available, they tend to avoid psychological approaches to the patient's illness entirely.

This trend was present even in Freud's day, as he noted in his article on mental treatment:

> [From all the] advances and discoveries . . . related to the physical side of man . . . it followed, as a result of an incorrect though easily understandable train of thought, that physicians tended to restrict their interest to the physical side of things and were glad to leave the mental field to be dealt with by the philosophers whom they despised.
>
> [18, p. 284]

Since Freud wrote this over a hundred years ago, the scope and power of scientific medicine has continued to grow, and as a result of its ever more impressive successes, scientific physical approaches to the patient now dominate medical thought even more than in his day. One consequence of this is that the mental approach to physical disease that Freud described in his article now seems quaint, archaic and even a bit pathetic. Even a mental approach to *mental* problems seems in the eyes of many today to be only a regrettable and temporary necessity. The part of medical practice that constituted mental treatment (in Freud's sense of "treatment that is aimed immediately and directly at the mind") has not developed alongside scientific physical medicine because the mental aspect of human illness does not lend itself to systematic scientific investigation. Rats have a physiology that is very close to that of humans, and they respond to disease in many of the same ways as humans. A rat model of human disease may therefore be quite relevant to human disease, and diseased rats may be used to study new treatments under controlled experimental conditions. But the psyches of rats are so far from those of humans that it has been impossible to find a rat model of anything but the most banal and uninteresting aspects of human mental life. Psychologists who have studied humans experimentally have been able to apply the formal rigor of modern science only to the understanding of human behavior, but have by and large failed to produce useful models of the human mind, either in health or disease. Moreover, mental treatments are too complex and variable (as is their target, the human mind) to lend themselves well to controlled clinical trials designed to establish their therapeutic efficacy.

These neglected aspects of medicine have been known traditionally as the art of medicine, the physician's informal and intuitive use of psychological means to influence the course of the patient's illness. While the modern physician's physical approach to the patient has become more refined, sensitive and sophisticated as a result of the impressive developments in the science of medicine, the physician's mental approach has become more and more crude, insensitive and unsophisticated as a result of the withering of the art of medicine.[1]

---

1 While I cannot go into it here in detail, I believe this fact is related to the current loss of trust in physicians and dissatisfaction with medical care that has reached troubling proportions in the United States, where the technological aspect of medical practice has come to so dominate its personal (or mental) aspect.

Should we care? If, as many believe, what were for centuries regarded as psychological components of illness will turn out to be physical after all, i.e., simply manifestations of brain physiology, and if physical medicine has on its side the enormous power of empirical science, does it really matter if the old "art" of medicine continues to wither? From this perspective, it is little more than handholding necessitated by inadequate physical treatment, and if physicians can root out the causes of illness through physical treatment, in the long run there will not be many hands that need to be held anyway.

Freud and the art of medicine

But before deciding that Freud's ideas on mental treatment belong in the dustbin of history, it might be worthwhile to examine more closely what they actually are. His thinking on mental treatment falls into two quite distinct phases.

The first was in one important respect much in line with the modern idea that scientific medicine can (and should) replace the old art of medicine. During this phase, Freud claimed to have developed a psychological treatment that could act not just in the non-specific, palliative way of the traditional art of medicine, but also, when properly administered, as a specific, radical, systematic and substantial treatment of mental illness. He claimed furthermore that this new treatment had a scientifically testable rationale, just like scientifically derived physical treatments, and that its effectiveness could likewise be tested scientifically.

In other words, he claimed that he had come up with a scientific human psychology that bore the same relationship to the mind that the science of physiology bore to the body, and that from this new scientific psychology he could derive treatments that were not only effective, but also testable and verifiable experimentally. He believed he had extended the range of the science of medicine, with its therapeutic potency and specificity, its rational explanatory powers and its empirical verifiability, to cover the arena formerly occupied only by the palliative, generic and untestable art of medicine. He (like contemporary scientifically inclined physicians) believed that the old art of medicine would wither away once his new scientific discoveries took effect.

It is difficult to overestimate the boldness of this claim. He was not just proposing a new theory and treatment of a previously untreatable illness, like the contemporaneous introduction of mercury salts to treat syphilis. He was proposing a radical revision of the concept of the kind of illness that could be treated scientifically. A Viennese poet, Alfred von Berger, reviewing Freud's *Studies on Hysteria*, captured the boldness and weirdness of Freud's claim when he titled his article "Surgery of the Soul" [29].

Freud formulated this radical approach to mental disorders in his theory of the specific etiology of hysteria. Briefly, this was the notion that trauma had caused a blockade of libido and that psychoanalytic treatment "lanced the abscess" of blocked libido, allowed the long-delayed libidinal catharsis to occur, and thereby reestablished the patient's normal libidinal circulation, the blockage of which had been the root cause of the neurotic symptoms. When Freud presented this model of hysteria, along with the results of the psychoanalytic treatment of eighteen patients, to the Vienna Medical Society, Krafft-Ebing, the chair of the meeting, dismissed it as a "scientific fairy tale" [28, vol. 1, p. 263].

Hagiographers of Freud attribute this response to the supposed cultural resistance to psychoanalysis, against which Freud had to battle heroically and alone. But what was in dispute at the Medical Society meeting was not Freud's contention that he had produced improvement in his patients. Such improvements were known to occur in hysteria in response to a variety – a distressingly wide variety – of physical and mental approaches. Freud's medical colleagues were criticizing only his claim to have discovered a specific and radical psychological treatment of hysteria, based on a scientific model *that was completely analogous to accepted physiologic models of physical disease*. The claim that he had developed a scientific mental treatment for hysteria that was in all essentials analogous to the scientific treatment of physical disorders meant that what for thousands of years had been part of the art of medicine (and, as far as anyone could tell, was destined to remain an art permanently) had now been suddenly and totally folded into the science of medicine. How could such a claim not have been greeted with skepticism?

As it turned out, the skepticism was largely justified, and Freud himself eventually acknowledged that his specific etiological model of hysteria had far outrun the evidence available to support it. When his specific etiology of hysteria collapsed, so did his claim for a specific and scientifically based treatment of hysteria.

In retrospect, it is not hard to see that his etiologic model of hysteria was simply an ad hoc explanation, couched in scientific terms, of the therapeutic results he had obtained over a period of years, using the "cathartic" method that he had developed by trial and error with his older friend and colleague Josef Breuer. Such ad hoc explanations sound scientific, but aren't.

As Freud's claim to have proposed a valid scientific rationale for his "cathartic" treatment of hysteria has not withstood the test of time, neither has his claim to have developed specific treatments, analogous to specific medical treatments, for any of the illnesses he attempted to treat. The psychoanalytic treatment for hysteria, obsessional states, melancholia and any other condition that psychoanalysts treat is the same: psychoanalysis. (This has given rise to the jape, "The treatment is psychoanalysis. What's the illness?") Moreover, attempts to validate the effectiveness of psychoanalytic treatment in anything like a controlled scientific study have been uniformly disappointing (I don't mean the results of such studies have been negative, I mean that attempts to construct such studies have themselves been disappointing).

Freud had overreached when he claimed to have placed "mental treatment", the traditional psychological approach to illness that physicians had practiced for millennia in an informal and intuitive way, on the base of physiology. If he had stopped there, his work would perhaps now be honored by modern psychobiologists as a pioneering attempt to create a scientific physical account of the mind, an achievement they believe they are now on the verge of realizing. But he did not stop there.

Following the collapse of his "scientific psychology", he began to approach mental treatment from an altogether different direction. He began this second phase of work on mental treatment with a careful and penetrating study of exactly how it worked.

To pursue this study, he put his psychophysiologic program on hold. Having failed to fold the art of medicine into the scientific approach, he began to study the art that physicians had employed for millennia in their informal, intuitive (but not highly reflective) way until he grasped something important about its operating principles. Rather than merely using these principles as a therapeutic tool, a more efficient or systematic art of medicine, he used them as the starting point for the development of a fundamentally new and systematic technique for investigating the mind. He realized the art of medicine was a combination of suggestion and what he called unconscious transference, and he spent the last forty years of his life pursuing his investigation of how they worked. He never returned to his psychophysiology.

Because it is based on the systematic study of the art of medicine, and because art is not subject to experimental scientific investigation, psychoanalysis could not embody the essential features of an experimental science: its hypotheses are not testable by scientific experimentation, and its theories lack the predictive power of theories generated by controlled experimentation. Although they are not testable by ordinary scientific means, the observations that psychoanalysis yields have nonetheless turned out to be precise, detailed, empirical and specific. This is how it could become something the art of medicine never was: a tool for investigating the mind. In addition, psychoanalysis has the power to touch and alter people's emotional lives in ways that the old art of medicine cannot equal and that scientific medicine cannot even approach.

While the modern view would celebrate the first phase of Freud's work (his attempt to reduce the art of medicine to medical science) and discard the second phase (his development of the art of medicine) as unscientific, I consider the earlier work to be an oversimplified view of the mind tailored to fit the constraints of physiology. In contrast, his later work, although sacrificing theoretical and experimental rigor, created a tool, that, however rudimentary, at least does not underestimate the complexity of the mind, nor gloss over the differences between mind and body.

Once Freud gave up trying to squeeze the art of medicine into the framework of a physiology of the mind, he could approach the problem of how the art of medicine works and of how to use it as a sophisticated and systematic therapeutic and investigational method unconstrained by the methodology and logic of experimental physical science.

Psychoanalysis and its insecurities

This freedom from investigative constraint is the great virtue of psychoanalysis. It has also been its greatest social liability. Abandoning the methodology of experimental science that had been so successful in physical medicine, and whose prestige matched its success, meant accepting a precipitous fall in whatever expectations psychoanalysts might have had to win for themselves the respectability enjoyed by science and scientific medicine. If psychoanalysis is not a science like physiology or physical medicine, it no longer has any claim to be part of the medical or scientific mainstream.

Psychoanalysts (beginning with Freud) have been reluctant to accept the loss of prestige and security this exclusion entails. There is a tension running throughout Freud's work between the new kind of investigation of the mind that he had discovered and his desire for scientific respectability: one can see him again and again forging ahead apparently unconcerned that he was producing ideas that were undeniably weird, only to lose his nerve at some point and start trying to show how it's all really not so new, then forging ahead again and so on.[2]

The tension in psychoanalysis between boldness and the desire for respectability has never been resolved, and perhaps never can be. In itself, this is not such a bad thing. But it is hard to live with, and psychoanalysts have attempted to evade it by pretending that psychoanalysis is more scientifically domesticated than it really is. This has done considerable damage to the field itself.

We may see a small example of this damage by reviewing the passage quoted at the beginning of this chapter. The translation by James Strachey in *The Standard Edition of the Complete Works of Sigmund Freud* is as follows:

2 See Part One of my *Immaterial Facts* [13] for a fuller discussion of the two phases of Freud's work, as well as of the tension between them.

"Psyche" is a Greek word which may be translated "mind". Thus, "psychical treatment" means "mental treatment". The term might accordingly be supposed to signify "treatment of the pathological phenomena of mental life." This, however, is *not* its meaning. "Psychical treatment" denotes, rather, treatment taking its start in the mind, treatment (whether of mental or physical disorders) by measures which operate in the first instance and immediately upon the human mind.
[18, p. 283, original emphasis][3]

The German title of the article from which it was taken is "Psychische Behandlung (Seelenbehandlung)". *Psychische Behandlung* means "Mental Treatment". *Seele* should be translated as "soul", and *Seelenbehandlung* therefore as "treatment of the soul", if we could divest the word "soul" of its religious connotation. (Strachey simply dropped the second component of the article's title when he translated it.) Keeping this in mind, a more faithful translation of the passage would be:

Psyche is a Greek word that translates into the German *soul [Seele]*. Psychical treatment [*psychische Behandlung*] therefore means *soul treatment*. One might think that this is to be understood as: treatment of the pathological manifestations of the life of the soul [*Seelenlebens*]. This is, however, not the meaning of this word. Mental treatment means much more: treatment from the soul outward [*von der Seele aus*], treatment – whether of soul-disturbances [*seelischer Störungen*] or physical disturbances [*körperlicher Störungen*] – by means that

---

3 In the original:

Psyche ist ein griechisches Wort und lautet in deutscher Übersetzung *Seele*. Psychische Behandlung heißt demnach *Seelenbehandlung*. Man könnte also meinen, daß darunter verstanden wird: Behandlung der krankhaften Erscheinungen des Seelenlebens. Dies ist aber nicht die Bedeutung dieses Wort. Psychische Behandlung will vielmehr besagen: Behandlung von der Seele aus, Behandlung-seelischer oder körperichler Störungen-mit Mitteln, welche zunächst und unmittelbar auf das Seelische des Menschen einwerken.
[19, p. 289]

work directly and immediately on the human soul [das *Seelische des Menschen* – literally, "that which is soulish in humans"].

This is an example of the tendency of Strachey's English translation of Freud to couch his ideas in language that appears more precise and scientific than the original, a tendency that Bettelheim [2] has decried at length. It compounds Freud's own predilection to outfit his ideas with scientific clothing, and has, in a subtle but powerful way, conditioned the thinking of generations of English-speaking psychoanalysts.

While psychoanalysts from medical backgrounds have attempted to make psychoanalysis look more scientific than it is, analysts from academic backgrounds have tried to portray it as an outgrowth of some other equally familiar and domesticated discipline, such as philosophy (especially hermeneutics) or linguistics. In both cases, psychoanalysis ends up portrayed as something more familiar and tame than it actually is.

These misrepresentations of psychoanalysis have a number of motives. One is the desire to achieve a greater degree of certainty than psychoanalysis itself offers: portraying it as a science akin to other medical sciences creates the illusion that psychoanalysis can achieve the level of certitude, verifiability and replicability that they enjoy. Another motive is to reassure themselves that they are dealing with something that, first, is not itself weird, dangerous and unpredictable, and second, helps people cope with things that are. A third motive is the desire to portray it to the public as something safe and effective, like an FDA-approved drug. A fourth motive is the desire for respectability and prestige. The last two are directly related to anxieties about the marketability of psychoanalysis. But there is more to this than a simple desire for greater market share. All four stem from a need to find in psychoanalysis the promise of mitigating the impact of those aspects of life that can only be suffered: death, birth, love, hatred, ignorance and fear of the unfamiliar. But this security is clearly contrary to what psychoanalysis has to offer. Psychoanalysis in its proper sense does not provide illusions to help avoid suffering, but rather helps one to tolerate unavoidable suffering. Freud himself summed up the effect of psychoanalysis as transforming "hysterical misery into common human suffering" [9]. (He was using the word "suffering" here in its original sense of "tolerance".)

If psychoanalysis is distorted into something that appears to offer security against the suffering and uncertainties of life, it becomes the opposite of itself; it becomes more like neurosis, and therefore worthy of Karl Kraus's well-known indictment that it is the disease of which it pretends to be the cure.

Psychoanalysis in its undistorted form is not the disease, but the cure that ultimately strips one of neurotic security-inducing illusions, and thereby permits one, for better or worse, to suffer life itself.

5

PSYCHOANALYTIC OBSERVATION

When the physicist Heinrich Löwy asked Freud in 1930 to write a contribution for a collection of solutions to problems in science, Freud agreed at first to do so. But as he tried to compose his article, he found himself struggling so much with his response that he finally gave up. He wrote to Löwy: "in trying to find some suitable examples I have encountered strange and almost insuperable obstacles, as though certain procedures that can be expected from other fields of investigation could not be applied to my subject matter" [16, p. 395].

Freud had difficulty coming up with a good example of a scientific solution to a psychoanalytic problem because to do so would have meant discarding some of his deep and unwavering convictions about psychoanalysis. The first of these was that the discovery of the unconscious had swept aside all problems of psychology as previously formulated, which now needed to be reformulated in terms of the unconscious. The second was that knowledge of the unconscious can be gained only by a method of observation unlike that of experimental science: "within the methods of our work there is no place for the kind of experiment made by physicists and physiologists" [16, p. 395].

If Freud's hysteria theory of the 1890s, with its claim to have put the art of medicine on a firm scientific basis, sounded radical, these new ideas, developed after he abandoned his old theory of hysteria, were no less so. By the early 1900s he was claiming to have discovered something – the unconscious – whose role in the operation of the mind is so fundamental that all questions in psychology must be reformulated to take it into

41

account: what had previously been regarded as the mind was only a part of the mind – the conscious part – which merely floated on the surface of the unconscious. Trying to explain the activity of the conscious mind without reference to unconscious dynamics was like trying to account for the motions of a leaf floating on a stream without reference to the stream. Freud said, furthermore, that the unconscious part of the mind, crucial to understanding anything important about mental processes, was so utterly different from anything science had yet considered that no accepted scientific method was suited to investigate it.

It is easy to see why critics of psychoanalysis find this claim, taken in its stark simplicity, too farfetched to be taken seriously. Supporters of psychoanalysis have tended to respond to critics by becoming apologists, arguing that psychoanalysis really is a science like other sciences, merely an embryonic one whose eventual experimental validation is only a question of time. Other analysts have argued that the scientific status of psychoanalysis is moot, because it is really like some other well-established discipline such as hermeneutics or linguistics. Both approaches remove psychoanalysis from the radical position in which Freud placed it.[1]

The origins of psychoanalysis

Freud's most influential mentor was the French neurologist Jean-Martin Charcot. In his obituary of Charcot, Freud described him as

> no brooder, no thinker, but an artistically gifted nature, or as he himself put it, a *visuel*, a seer . . . He used to look again and again at things he did not understand, to deepen his impression of them day by day, till suddenly an understanding of them dawned on him. In his mind's eye the apparent chaos presented by the continual repetition of the same symptoms then gave way to order: the new nosological pictures emerged, characterized by

1 I have relied for many of the ideas in this chapter on the work of the Swiss psychoanalyst Giovanni Vassalli [36].

the constant combination of certain groups of symptoms. He might be heard to say that the greatest satisfaction a man could have was to see something new, that is, to recognize it as new.

[17, p. 11]

"New" here means not already known and understood. Freud's approach to understanding the mind, which followed Charcot's, was to observe the patient without a preconceived theory about the significance of what he was observing until a picture emerged. He arrived at this picture through inspiration, not reason. He avoided theoretical preconceptions, which tend to be general; that is, they tend to refer to types or classes of phenomena of which the present instance is an example. By deliberately keeping his theoretical preconceptions at bay, Freud protected his capacity to see what was new or unique about *this* patient from what he already knew about the *type* of patient he was dealing with.

Scientists also employ this kind of open observation and educated intuition to arrive at new theoretical ideas when they are dealing with areas about which very little is known. A well-documented example of this is Watson and Crick's inspired guess about the structure of DNA, based on data from X-ray crystallography.

But – and here is the crux of the difference between psychoanalysis and the experimental sciences – when scientists arrive at conjectures, they frame them in the form of hypotheses and design experiments to test them. Such experiments are precisely what Freud told Löwy he could find no place for in his work.

By the time he wrote *An Outline of Psychoanalysis* almost ten years after writing his letter to Löwy, Freud had ceded experiment even more explicitly to the natural sciences: "We have discovered technical methods of filling up the gaps in the phenomena of our consciousness, and we make use of those methods just as a physicist makes use of experiment" [24, pp. 196–7]. Here "just as" means "in place of". But what are these "technical methods"?

Before exploring this question, I would like to review the difficulty of the position Freud created for himself by rejecting the accepted principles of scientific medicine, a difficulty that he bequeathed intact to his professional heirs. Freud had no lack of appreciation for the profound scientific revolution in physical medicine that had begun in his lifetime. Still, following the collapse of his ideas about the specific etiology of hysteria, he had no inclination to treat the mind as something that could be explained entirely by reference to physiologic processes (a trend that continues to this day to be the subject of fierce philosophical debate). On the contrary, as we have seen, his great discoveries stemmed not from his interest in the mind as an epiphenomenon of physiology, but from his exploration of how "mental treatment" worked, regardless of physiology.

Freud knew that the ancient tradition of mental treatment (that is, treatment based on an appreciation of the influence of the mind on the patient's physical well-being, and of the possibility of the physician's influencing the mind directly and through it the body indirectly) had languished during the period of the development of scientific physical medicine. Once "scientific" medicine established itself as a predominant force, the idea of the mind in its own right, as a subject independent of physical processes, began to look like an embarrassing indulgence in a quaint Romantic sensibility. The problem for analysts has been to show that psychoanalysis is not just a sophisticated expression of late Viennese Romanticism, like the music of Mahler and Strauss. But, as Vassalli [36, pp. 6–7] put it, "the pressure and impatience of the time led to generations of analysts after Freud generally resolving this Gordian knot by simply cutting through it" – declaring psychoanalysis to be a part of science.

Official declarations aside, the fact remains that by postulating the existence of a hidden daemonic force that he christened the Unconscious, Freud appeared to be engaging in Romantic fantasies; by claiming to be able to discern through a kind of heightened sensitivity what was unconscious in his patients, he appeared to be claiming that he could read minds; and by claiming to be able to influence the mind with words, he appeared to be engaging in the use of magic.

Freud's technique

How accurate are these appearances? Freud did not believe in mind-reading. In a paper on mental treatment, he discusses psychic mediums:

what is known as "thought-reading" [*Gedanken erraten*] may be explained by small, involuntary muscular movements carried out by the "medium" in the course of an experiment – when, for instance, he has to make someone discover a hidden object [without giving any ostensible prompting]. The whole phenomenon might be more suitably described as "thought-betraying" [*Gedanken verraten*].

[18, p. 288]

Vassalli [36] says that the play on the words *verraten* (betraying) and *erraten* (guessing) points to a basic dynamic that Freud used in his technique. Freud relied on information that the patient betrayed (intentionally or not) in order to make "guesses" about what is in the patient's mind though unknown to the patient. This information is conveyed to the analyst through nonverbal communications such as body language, the intonation and music of speech, and through verbal cues such as the sequence of the patient's associations, and observations of what might normally have been said but was not, at a certain point in the session.

Freud believed that the analyst had to "more or less divine" what was operating unconsciously in the patient. He believed that a correct guess allowed the patient to articulate with feeling what was in his unconscious. "The situation may be compared with the unlocking of a locked door, after which opening it by turning the handle offers no further difficulty" [9].

A technique of guessing may provide inspired insights, but it will not provide anything close to a coherent theory. Freud did not apologize for this lack of coherence. As he wrote in *Studies on Hysteria*:

I am making use here of a number of similes, all of which have only a very limited resemblance to my subject and which, moreover, are incompatible with one another. I am aware that this is so, and I am in no danger of over-estimating their value. But my purpose in using them is to throw light from different directions on a highly complicated topic which has never yet been represented. I shall therefore venture in the following

45

pages to introduce similes in the same manner, though I
know this is not free from objection.

[9, p. 291]

Freud's *sang-froid* about theoretical coherence has stirred up
doubts in the minds of analysts (as well as others) about the
legitimacy of psychoanalysis. But instead of addressing these
doubts directly, analysts have officially evaded them. We can see
the evidence of this evasion in the contrast between Freud's
definition of psychoanalysis and the official definition of today.
In 1923, Freud defined psychoanalysis as follows:

> Psychoanalysis is the name (1) of a procedure for the
> investigation of mental processes which are almost
> inaccessible in any other way, (2) of a method (based on
> that investigation) for the treatment of neurotic dis-
> orders and (3) of a collection of psychological infor-
> mation obtained along these lines, which is gradually
> being accumulated into a new scientific discipline.
>
> [22, p. 235]

Compare this with a recent definition of psychoanalysis formulated by a committee of the International Psychoanalytic
Association (IPA):

> The term "psychoanalysis" refers to a theory of person-
> ality structure and function and to a specific psycho-
> therapeutic technique. This body of knowledge is based
> on and derived from the fundamental psychological
> discoveries made by Sigmund Freud.
>
> (IPA Membership Handbook and Roster 2001,
> pp. 27–8, Article 3)

While in Freud's definition, the method of investigation gives
rise to the method of treatment as well as to "a collection of
psychological information", the IPA definition leaps from a
collection of information to "a theory of personality structure
and function". This reverses Freud's priorities. As Vassalli
points out:

46

This epistemic reversal has brought psychoanalysis since Freud into a fundamentally different position [that] seems to justify the conclusion that it is no longer a question of "building out into the dark", but of the assertion of a methodological premise for which certainty and evidence are the most important criteria. The historical consequences of this adaptation are immense and a completely different light would be shed on many contemporary questions about psychoanalytic science if this background were taken into account.

[36, p. 19]

Techne

Vassalli compares the method that Freud employed in place of scientific experimentation to *techne*, a term the ancient Greeks used for the process required for the practical production of a specific object. *Techne* has the same root as the modern words technique and technology, but it denotes something quite different. One can learn a technique, and, having learned it, may apply it in a more or less mechanical way to achieve a preconceived goal. Techniques are tricks of the trade. *Techne* is more like the work of a sculptor, where the goal is not clear at the beginning, but emerges during the process of creation. It is not a rule to be followed, but a kind of learning, one that extracts knowledge from an examination of the unique process required (but unknown beforehand) to produce a result. If techniques are tricks of the trade, *techne* is improvisation followed by a study of how one had improvised the specific task at hand.

Techne does not just provide the opportunity to learn about the problem as one tries to solve it, it demands that one learn approaches tailored to the unique and specific problem at hand. These approaches have to be developed ad hoc. They cannot be codified for subsequent application to future problems (although they may be used in the future, if the analyst finds on an ad hoc basis that they are appropriate to the new problem). Whatever knowledge one gains from this activity must, in Freud's words, "fall into one's house as uninvited

guests while one is occupied with the investigation of details"
[26, p. 83].

This kind of investigation yields knowledge that does not
have the certainty we associate with well-established scientific
theories. An analyst working with a patient is like an artist
exploring the aesthetic potential of a new medium – with a
crucial difference: whereas artists mold their material in a
process that expresses their vision, the analyst's "vision" for the
patient is an entirely subordinate and dispensable part of the
analysis. The analyst's interpretations are far less important
than the patient's response to them. Where artists try to produce
something by molding their material, analysts try to understand
the nature of their material (the patient's mind), by making an
interpretation *and then observing the response*, compared to
which the interpretation itself is of minor importance. An
interpretation is not an attempt to mold the patient, but a device
for sounding his depths. It acts more like a question than an
answer.

The proper empirical method for exploring the inanimate
world is controlled experimentation, while the proper empirical
method for exploring the animate world of the mind is hunch-
based reasoning. The kinds of language appropriate for
describing each of these worlds are as different as the methods
for exploring them.

When describing the inanimate world, words convey information about mechanics, and the kind of precision and
accuracy that is important in the use of such words is a
mechanical one. Describing the animate world, on the other
hand, calls for a different kind of language, one whose precision
and accuracy is poetic rather than mechanical. It may sound
strange to talk of poetry as precise and accurate, but consider
how Shakespeare with only a few words was able to say
precisely what a whole page of scientifically exact description
only circles around.

Furthermore, when we act on the inanimate world, we do so
with inanimate (mechanical) means. But when we act on someone's mind, we do so by communicating meaning – an animate
means of action. Poetic language is not only the most compact
and accurate means of describing states of mind, it has the
greatest power to evoke and to move the mind.

48

The relationship of treatment and research in psychoanalysis

Freud claimed that in psychoanalysis, research and treatment coincide precisely when he wrote that, " it was impossible to treat a patient without learning something new", and "it was impossible to gain fresh insight without perceiving its beneficent result" [23, p. 256].

But this beneficial research is not the kind that leads to theoretical generalization. It is *techne*. Freud wrote in 1912 that

one of the claims of psychoanalysis to distinction is, no doubt, that in its execution research and treatment coincide; nevertheless, after a certain point, the technique required for the one opposes that required for the other. It is not a good thing to work on a case scientifically while treatment is still proceeding – to piece together its structure, to try to foretell its further progress, and to get a picture from time to time of the current state of affairs, as scientific interest would demand. Cases which are devoted from the first to scientific purposes and are treated accordingly suffer in their outcome; while the most successful cases are those in which one proceeds, as it were, without any purpose in view, allows oneself to be taken by surprise by any new turn in them, and always meets them with an open mind, free from any presuppositions.

[20, p. 114]

The scientific interest that demands that one "piece together its structure, to try to foretell its further progress, and to get a picture from time to time of the current state of affairs" is, of course, scientific interest in the sense of theoretical abstraction – "not a good thing," according to Freud – while proceeding without any purpose in view, allowing oneself to be taken by surprise by any new turn of event, always meeting them with an open mind, free from any presuppositions and from the need to predict, yields "the most successful outcomes" – and is a precise description of *techne*.

49

Discussion

If Freud's whole enterprise is based on guessing or hunches rather than on experience embodied in an applicable theoretical canon, it becomes critically important for the analyst to be able to tell the difference between apposite guessing and ordinary wild speculation. Apposite guessing is more or less accurate because it is based on something that already exists in the patient's unconscious mind. Wild speculation is based on something that exists in the *analyst's* mind, not in the patient's.

It is also crucial to distinguish between legitimate interpretation, which is meant only to convey information to the patient about himself, and suggestion or propaganda, which is meant to *alter* the patient's mind in some specific and directed way. The magic of words works its effect on the mind regardless of the truth of what is being suggested.

These two crucial distinctions converge around the issue of truth. To what degree are analysts able to perceive the truth about their patient, and to what degree are they able to let that truth exist unmolested, to simply describe it without attempting to sell the patient a "cure"? I have previously suggested [10] that a psychoanalytic interpretation should not be an attempt to cure the patient of anything (except perhaps unconscious self-deception); it should only be a communication about the patient's state of mind.

The truths that emerge in an analysis are not difficult to understand once we see them, but they are difficult to see because they have been obscured. The truth is generally evident if nothing interferes with our view of it. This is a big "if", however, and it is highly unlikely that we can ever evade such interference completely. This is just a way of saying that there is such a thing as the truth, that we are able to perceive it, but that our perception of it is always imperfect.

The problem we face is how to make our capacity to see the truth as perfect as practicable. The solution must be to reduce, as much as possible, whatever it is that interferes with our view of it. It would be impossible to catalogue everything that interferes with our capacity to see the truth in analysis, but in general, the obstacles seem to fall into the category of wishes: wishes that an analyst has for himself and his patient, wishes that a patient has for himself and his analyst, and wishes they both have about the nature of their relationship. It is a paradox of analysis that the only way to conduct one properly is to abandon all hope that it will turn out as one wishes. Only then can our capacity to see the truth be free of interference from our wishes.

Complete freedom from wishes, conscious or unconscious, is not possible. There can be no guarantee that what analysts perceive will be accurate and complete, nor that what they say will be entirely untendentious. Fortunately, it does not need to be. We only need to make our understanding of the situation in analysis *relatively* more free – a little freer than it was the last time. And then to make it even a little more free the next time.

It is conceivable that it is not the truth that is therapeutic in psychoanalysis, but rather the habit of mind associated with the pursuit of truth – a habit of mind that recognizes one's wishes and the needs they express, acknowledges them as quite real, but does not confuse them with realities other than themselves.

6

ROOM FOR DOUBT

If you look at a dog following the advice of his nose, he
traverses a patch of land in a completely unplottable
manner. And he invariably finds what he is looking for.
W.G. Sebald

If the ability to follow one's nose depends on freedom from
presuppositions, wishes, preconceptions and theoretical invest-
ment, or, to put it another way, on the ability to pursue hunches
or "build out into the dark", then the ability to doubt what one
knows (or rather what one thinks one knows) would seem to be
close to the heart of the matter. Hand in hand with room for
doubt and healthy skepticism goes a free imagination – the
ability *seriously* to consider all possibilities, unfettered by preconceptions. And as initial skepticism is necessary for a free
imagination, a free imagination is required for firm convictions.
I will try to illustrate this point with some clinical examples.

The first concerns a patient in a middle management position
in a large corporation who caught a subordinate filing a false
expense account claim.

The patient reported this incident to his supervisor (as company
policy required), who issued a mild reprimand to the subordinate.
The patient was terribly upset by what he considered to be the
inappropriate mildness of the subordinate's punishment; it was the
latest in a series of episodes that indicated to him the corporate
administration's lack of willingness to back up its managers in their

53

efforts to maintain ethical standards. He made an appointment with his supervisor, but later became anxious and tried to cancel the appointment. The supervisor insisted that they meet.

Reluctantly, the patient began to tell the supervisor how he felt about the way things had been going at the company, and expressed his view that the corporate administration had sunk to the level of "gutter ethics". At one point, the patient said something – he couldn't recall exactly what, but remembered he had felt very heated – and his supervisor told him that if he didn't know the patient was his friend, and didn't realize how upset the patient was, he'd be insulted by what the patient had said. He then explained to the patient the pressures the company was under from litigious employees and hungry attorneys. The patient felt grateful for the information, and for his supervisor's willingness to discuss things calmly with him. He thanked him and left feeling that he and his supervisor had reached a much better mutual understanding.

But when he arrived home that day, he felt terribly exhausted and fell immediately into a deep sleep – like a coma, as he later described it. He awoke extremely depressed. He said he could not recall ever feeling so depressed before, and that the depression had been so severe it frightened him. He was convinced he had ruined things for himself permanently at the company, despite what he consciously knew. When recounting this for me, he said that he could not get around the feeling that he had ruined his life. As it turned out, the supervisor's attitude toward the patient was benign, and the patient had done no damage to his life or career.

Although he was consciously aware of the fact that things were not so bad between himself and his supervisor, he experienced this awareness as something like a counterintuitive conclusion that one might arrive at through a process of logical deduction: if he focussed on the facts and went over the logic, he had to accept the conclusion, but it just didn't feel right.

Consider this possibility: while this patient could observe the supervisor's attitude and reason his way to a realistic conclusion about his status, he could not really imagine that such a situation could be so. Therefore, what he knew was not available to him in a practical way: he couldn't really believe what he knew.

Psychoanalysts have observed for many years that for the insight provided by a good interpretation to become useful in a practical sense, for conviction or belief about it to exist, something more than intellectual awareness is needed. Intellectual awareness rests on the surface of the mind, while one's convictions and beliefs operate below the surface to shape how one feels things are, as opposed to what one thinks they are. For knowledge to be felt as well as known, one needs a pliant imagination. The capacity to know and to use any observation in a practical way depends on being able first to imagine that it might be true not just as an abstract idea, but as a real possibility.

Imagination provides us with the range of possibilities we can consider. It is the wellspring for the scientist's hypotheses, and also for the hypotheses of everyday life.

Imaginative conjectures that are capable of serving as hypotheses must be able to be subordinated to evidence. To use a grammatical analogy, they must be questions, not statements – not "such-and-such is happening", but "I think such-and-such may be happening. Is it?" If the hypothesis is genuinely a question, it may be answered by evidence. A "no" makes possible the search for alternate hypotheses to which the answer might be "yes". But even an immediate "yes" only raises further questions which could not even have been asked if the hypothesis hadn't been tried out. Any advance in our knowledge of the world not only tells us something we didn't know, but also suggests possibilities we hadn't imagined. Just as imagination allows us to make sense out of our observations, new observations also foster our imagination.

Imaginative hypotheses must be capable of being linked to something outside themselves, such as other hypotheses, subjective experiences or sensory perceptions, without which they are incomplete. Knowledge that makes a difference – knowledge that may be used as a basis of action and decision – is created by the linking of imaginative conjectures with experience.

Using the analogy of chemical compounds, Wilfred Bion devised the term "unsaturated" to describe such imaginative ideas. An unsaturated chemical molecule is one on which there are points to which other molecules may bond to form a complex molecule. Molecules to which other molecules cannot link because their binding sites are completely occupied are called "saturated".

Imaginative hypotheses that are useful in the creation of practical knowledge are unsaturated – they are questions with sites to which new ideas may attach. Saturated ideas are statements that assert not what might be true, but what had *better* be true, and they are not useful parts of empirical investigation. Saturated ideas are held not because they are useful investigatory tools, or because empirical evidence supports them, but because they provide a feeling of security in the face of uncontrolled experience.[1] Terror of the unknown drives people to saturated ideas and to claim they are not open to question.

Saturated ideas inhibit the unsaturated imagination that is necessary for learning from experience. I can perhaps illustrate this with an example from the analysis of a second patient, an attorney who retired from the practice of law to raise a family.

She arrived at her session one Tuesday and said she was tired, as she had gotten to bed late because she had waited for her husband to get off the Internet, which she resented. She then said she had a lunch date "with some ladies" she wasn't looking forward to, and after that had to help her daughter with school science projects, which she also wasn't looking forward to because in the past she had ended up doing the science projects herself. But, she added with a distinct air of resignation, "It's OK".

I said she sounded like she was describing a lot of stuff she had to do but didn't like, but that it was all OK. With an air of finality and resignation, she said, "That's about it. I just have to keep my head down and get through it. It'll all be over by Thursday. I don't think I'm having a very good session".

I said that she knew from previous sessions that if she was open to the analysis, it often made her have strong feelings, including some she didn't want to have and couldn't control. And I suggested that she might feel better off keeping her head down and being mildly

---

1 These ideas correspond to what Freud called omnipotent thinking.

discontented in the session than risking something more powerful and perhaps quite unpleasant.

She replied that I was being critical and hostile.

I asked her, "What if I'm not? What if your decision is really OK with me?" She said she didn't know. I asked her to imagine what she'd feel. She said she guessed it would mean I was indifferent and uncaring. So either I was hostile and critical, or I was indifferent and uncaring.

The patient literally could not seriously imagine an attitude on my part of concerned, respectful objectivity. She took the feeling that I was either hostile or indifferent as a fact – as the only imaginable possibility, in fact – and it prevented her from being able to imagine anything else.

To imagine anything else would have left her too anxious, because she desperately needed someone who was concerned, respectful and objective. On those occasions when she felt that someone like that was available, she experienced feelings whose power made her unbearably anxious. The fact that the feelings were positive did not make their power any more bearable.

Even to imagine that I was concerned, thoughtful, respectful and objective would have presented this patient with a possibility that terrified her. By excluding that possibility from her repertoire of imaginable conjectures, she precluded the development in her mind of a terrifying scenario. The exclusion constricted her ability to think. She was literally scared out of her wits. She shielded herself from terror by clinging to a saturated view of things that, however depressing, unrealistic and hopeless, was familiar and tolerable.

Saturated ideas carry a sense of conviction that is greater than that derived from ordinary knowledge, which is subject to questions and doubts. They are like sacred beliefs, having nothing to do with experience or evidence. The sway they exert derives from their power to relieve anxiety.

The need to evade anxiety prevents us from even imagining that certain ideas might or might not be true, and produces a poverty of imagination. An impoverished imagination cannot provide the hypotheses needed to learn from experience.

A free imagination can lead to a sense of conviction that is secure because the ideas it generates may be supported by evidence. Omniscience produces convictions that are insecure because they must constantly fend off evidence. This insecurity is apparent from the fact that even though people who hold such convictions express complete confidence in their solidity, they act (quite rightly) as though these convictions were fragile. They do not welcome experiences that might challenge or constrain their beliefs. In contrast, people who entertain genuine imaginative hypotheses tend to welcome challenges to their beliefs, since a belief will either survive the challenge, which will strengthen it, or it will not, which will stimulate a search for a modified hypothesis that will.

One of the criteria for having an imagination in good operating condition is the capacity to imagine alternative hypotheses – to doubt what one imagines or believes to be the case, without excessive anxiety. Those who begin with certainties end with doubt, while those who begin with doubt end with (relative) certainty.

Saturation, unsaturation and the unconscious

In his *Introductory Lectures on Psychoanalysis* [21], Freud, trying to describe what it means for something to be unconscious, wrote that he believed the dreamer knows the unconscious meaning of his dream, but does not know that he knows it, and for that reason thinks that he does not know it. However, having an unconscious idea is not just the ordinary case of knowing something without knowing one knows it. Socrates claimed that even a slave boy who had never heard of the Pythagorean Theorem might still be said to "know" it, because he could lead the child through the entire proof step by step, without introducing him to any information he did not already possess. But if Socrates had been trying to teach something that was unconscious in the psychoanalytic sense, the boy still will not have known it (like the patient in my first example) even after Socrates had demonstrated that he did. Or rather, he would have known it only intellectually: he would know it, but still act and feel as though it weren't true. We can know things without believing them – without feeling the truth of what we know. Freud called this phenomenon repression.

When we attempt to confront something repressed, we find ourselves suddenly afflicted with a peculiar kind of learning disability. Our ability to know in a practical way what is in our own minds is limited because the apparatus we have for observing and articulating certain kinds of experiences has been damaged. I propose that this damage may take the form of an inability freely to entertain imaginative conjectures about what we are looking at. Such conjectures are relevant to the experience at hand (one must be able to imagine that something might be true before one can learn it is), and they can join with the experience or perception at hand (in the sense that a scientific conjecture or hypothesis joins with data).

If the mental space a conjecture needs to occupy in order to link with experience has already been occupied by an omniscient belief, the conjecture cannot be entertained. It is therefore not available for linking with experience. The result is that both observation of and learning from experience are blocked.

Such blockage of mental space by omniscient beliefs is hardly rare. Bion suggested that it should be suspected whenever anyone provides an explanation for anything:

> People do not often deliberately and consciously with-
> hold information when they are expected to provide it.
> That would be a conscious example of presenting the
> inquirer with a blank space. There are, however, certain
> failures to answer which Freud considers to be
> unconsciously withheld – that is, they are not deliberate
> attempts at falsification, deception, and evasion. There
> are other occasions when a person . . . presents an
> answer that seems to be unsatisfactory. Freud calls this
> false memory, intended to fill the space left empty by the
> amnesia. This suggestion is fruitful: it leads to more
> questions and inquiries which I would tend still further.
> If it is true that the human being, like nature, abhors a
> vacuum, cannot tolerate empty space, then he will try to

fill it by finding something to go into that space presented by his ignorance. The intolerance of frustration, the dislike of being ignorant, the dislike of having a space which is not filled, can stimulate a precocious and premature desire to fill the space. One should therefore always consider that our theories, including the whole of psycho-analysis, psychiatry, medicine, are simply a kind of space-filling elaboration. In other words, the practising analyst has to decide whether he is promulgating a theory, or a space-filler.

[7, p. 229]

Thinking and feeling

The displacement of an imaginative conjecture by a space-filling belief produces not only a learning (thinking) disorder, but also a feeling disorder. An imaginative conjecture is not just an idea, it is an idea that is invested with, and derived from, emotion. Without imaginative conjectures, we have no emotionally laden ideas to match with or adopt experience, and consequently no feelings about the meaning of our experiences. By displacing imagination, omniscience obstructs both feeling and understanding, and allows one to acquire only experience or understanding that is intellectually constricted and emotionally cut off.

One of the specific tasks of psychoanalysis is to reverse the type of damage to the apparatus for learning from experience that omniscient beliefs produce. Psychoanalysis helps patients to unsaturate saturated beliefs, thereby opening a space in the mind into which experience may be admitted. This process restores to patients their powers of observation and hence their ability to learn from their experiences, their capacity to know what is true and to feel what it means.

Psychoanalytic interpretation

Someone in emotional contact with another person may be able to sense something about that person's state of mind on his own, independent of what the other person says about it. What he senses (or guesses or intuits) may correlate with what the other person can tell him about his state of mind, but it may also supplement it or even contradict it. This fact raises an interesting question: if an outside observer can really supplement or even contradict what someone is aware of about his own state of mind, how does he do it? He must be in contact with the other person's mind by a route different from that by which the other person himself has access. Certainly there are aspects of our own minds that we simply cannot observe at a given moment, even though they may be apparent later, or may have been apparent earlier. But the fact that we are not in contact with an inner state does not prevent someone else from being in contact with it. In other words, the unconscious exists and it can be interpreted.

We all suffer at times from what might be called a focal learning disability. An aphorism in clinical medicine says that any diagnosis is easy to make once you think of it. Every clinician has had the experience of seeing something that makes sense out of a previously puzzling clinical problem, something that suddenly appears to be so obvious that we cannot understand why we didn't see it immediately. In retrospect, the problem does not appear to be complex or even particularly new. When this happens, it feels as if we have recovered from some sort of intellectual disability.

We bear the same relationship to ourselves: our ability to observe ourselves and to articulate these observations can become so attenuated that another person at times – almost any other person – is able to know how we feel better than we do.

Keeping in mind the limits of our powers of observation along with the fundamental importance of unsaturation and room for doubt, we can arrive at certain rough, general criteria for useful psychoanalytic interpretations.

First, psychoanalytic interpretations are descriptions of another person's state of mind that are derived from emotional contact with that person.

Second, a psychoanalytic interpretation must refer to something that patients are in a position to observe for themselves. To the degree that an interpretation derives from a source other than immediate, real-time contact with the patient (such as the analyst's theories, empirical studies of other patients who have been classed together with the current patient, the patient's history, the analyst's desire to cure the patient, memories of past contacts with the patient, and so on), it will not be about something that the patient is in a position to observe for himself at the moment. The patient can therefore not subject it to his own critical judgment about its status as something real or true, but can only yield to it or reject it. In other words, such an interpretation is, from the patient's point of view, not susceptible to being tested by experience, and can only be either accepted on authority, or dismissed.

Third, an interpretation is only an opinion. Although emotional contact places the analyst in a position to observe the patient's inner states, it is important to remember that emotional contact is not mind reading. Contact with another person's inner states is inherently indirect and complex. We can only read signs and form an opinion. And since the contact we have with our own minds is similarly complex and indirect, our observations about our own minds are not perfect. We can only read signs and form opinions about ourselves. There is no reason to privilege the analyst's interpretation over the patient's – or vice versa. To be effective, interpretations must be freely given and taken in an atmosphere of exploration.

Fourth, an interpretation, being an observation, is a description, not a prescription. It is a communication about how something is, not how it should be.

Finally, psychoanalytic interpretations must be made in an atmosphere of doubt about their meaning. An ideal observation starts off being meaningless: as Paul Valèry put it, "seeing is forgetting the name of the thing you're looking at".[2] Psychoanalytic interpretations consist of observations about the patient's internal experiences – not of explanations about what these observations mean. In fact, the psychoanalytic value of observations is diminished by explanations intended to make what has been observed logically coherent, since such explanations saturate the observation and prevent the formation of valid, spontaneous links between observations, which arise unexpect-

2 This is a loose translation of "Oublier insensiblement la chose que l'on regarde. L'oublier en y pensant, par une transformation naturelle . . . retrouver la chose" (*Varieté*, p. 244). Lawrence Weschler used it in the title of his book *Seeing is Forgetting the Name of the Thing One Sees: A Life of Contemporary Artist Robert Irwin* (University of California Press, Berkeley, CA, 1982).

edly from the observations themselves. An observation does not need coherence or rational explanation. Furthermore, if its meaning is to be discovered (as opposed to invented), the observation itself must first be considered meaningless. Bion discusses this point in his book *Transformations*:

> Since the first requisite for the discovery of meaning of any conjunction [observation] depends on the ability to admit that the phenomena may have no meaning, an inability to admit that they have no meaning stifles the possibility of curiosity at the outset.
>
> [6, p. 81]

In a letter to Ferenczi in August 1915 (quoted in [26]), Freud wrote: "I consider that one should not make theories. They should arrive unexpectedly in your house, like a stranger one hasn't invited." Similarly, analysts should not make explanations – they should arrive unexpectedly, like uninvited strangers. Although surprise and strangeness are not often signs of logical coherence, they clinically signal what might be called psychoanalytic coherence – a state of mind in which something old might be leading to something new.

Observation and articulation

An intolerance of meaninglessness and a need for premature coherence pose serious dangers to the capacity to observe and discover. Freud defended his use of incompatible similes to describe this state of affairs in "The Psychotherapy of Hysteria" [9], by pointing out that his purpose was to "throw light from different directions on a highly complicated topic which has never yet been represented". An interpretation is supposed to describe not something already known, and not even something merely unknown, but something unconscious – something that has (at least from the point of view of the patient's conscious experience) not yet been represented (or perhaps may have once been experienced and later repressed or split off). Repressed or split-off experiences are not simply forgotten. They are forgotten along with means for representing (observing and articulating) them, including the relevant unsaturated imagination. If the means of representing what has been repressed have been destroyed, analysis must not only describe what has been repressed: it must also restore the imaginative means of representing (observing and articulating) something unconscious. Until then, the unconscious idea is still for practical purposes something "never yet represented".

The therapeutic effect of psychoanalysis

In the view I am proposing here, the goal of clinical psychoanalysis is only to help patients arrive at a position in which they can observe and articulate their own internal experiences, and therefore find out for themselves who they are and what they mean. Psychoanalysis does not aim to change, modify or improve who patients are, nor even to tell them who they are; it only gets them into a position to find out for themselves. The only growth that psychoanalysis produces in patients' personality is in the area of their capacity to make observations about their internal experiences: feelings, intuitions and senses.[3]

In other words, while psychoanalysis may not increase patients' understanding of themselves, it does something far more important: it increases patients' capacity to observe in the absence of an understanding of what they have observed – their capacity for mental unsaturation. Of all psychological and psychopharmacological therapies, only psychoanalysis can do this. The capacity for unsaturation – the ability to tolerate doubts and uncertainty – is not a luxury enjoyed by especially keen observers, but a prerequisite for any type of observation at all. The capacity to observe is the capacity to observe without understanding.[4] The idea that psychoanalysis provides understanding and explanation is precisely wrong. It, and it alone among psychological therapies, offers the capacity to observe

---

3 Since part of everyone's internal experiences consists of the impact of other people, the capacity to observe one's internal experiences also implies the capacity to be in emotional contact with (to "read") others. Better contact with one's internal world also implies better contact with one's objects.

4 In Darwin's words, "It is a fatal fault to reason whilst observing, though so necessary beforehand and so useful afterwards" (*The Autobiography of Charles Darwin*, edited by Nora Barlow. Collins, London, 1958, p. 159).

without understanding so that meaning and understanding can emerge on their own, unobstructed by saturated ideas, including premature "understanding".

By enhancing the patient's capacity to observe without understanding, psychoanalysis places the patient in a better position to make his or her own observations, and, having made them, to allow whatever unexpected and unknown links that exist between them – their meaning – to emerge on their own into the patient's view.

7

PSYCHOANALYTIC REASONING

Finding the context

A "psychoanalytic statement", according to Wilfred Bion, is a statement made in the course of an analysis that is ultimately based on, and somehow communicates, an emotional experience.[1] Such a statement, which, according to Bion, can be "anything from an inarticulate grunt to quite elaborate constructions", expresses the emotional experience from which it derives. It bears the same relationship to that experience as a painting of a field of poppies does to a field of poppies [8]. This formulation is entirely comparable to the physical scientist's view that hypotheses or theories are legitimate to the degree that they describe the physical evidence. The difference, of course, is that, whereas in physical science what counts as evidence are sensory perceptions, in psychoanalysis what counts as evidence are emotional perceptions.

Bion later elaborated his idea of "psychoanalytic statements" into that of "psychoanalytic elements" [5], which consist of three parts: a sensory component (ordinary sensory representations, like the images that appear in a dream), passion, and a "mythological" component (which refers to the fact that a psychoanalytic element is part of a narrative that conveys a psychological truth).

---

1 This chapter is an expanded version of my review of Wilfred Bion's *Taming Wild Thoughts* [12].

A story by the journalist Tim Rutten [34] about Samuel Beckett illustrates the nature of the "mythological" component of a psychoanalytic element:

> Beckett used to pause occasionally to torment academics hoping to discover precisely what had inspired him to write "Waiting for Godot" with its two tramps, Vladimir and Estragon. (He said to Susan Sontag, among others, that the play actually originated in the "vertigo and nausea" he experienced during the agonizing waits entailed by his work for the French Resistance.)
>
> The playwright told more than one professor, though, that, at a certain point in his life, he'd spent a great deal of time in the Bibliothèque Nationale in Paris reading Augustine.
>
> There he had come across the saint's reflection on the two thieves the Gospels say were crucified on either side of Christ. He was struck, Beckett said, by the theologian's admonition: "Do not despair, one of the thieves was saved. Do not presume, one of the thieves was damned."
>
> But, as the medievalist and Augustine scholar James J. O'Donnell recently pointed out, "Thinking of Vladimir and Estragon as the two thieves crucified with Jesus is intriguing, to say the least, and it is wonderfully Beckett-like that the particular passage cannot be found anywhere in the surviving writings of Augustine . . . for all that the language and tenor are quite perfectly Augustinian."
>
> In other words, an insight delivered with perfect pitch, and achingly true – but in what sense?

Recognizing what Bion called the mythological component of the patient's communication means assuming that what the patient says is true – even achingly true – in some sense, and that it is the analyst's job to answer the question, "in what sense?" – that is, in what context?

The work of analysis consists of an approach that is unsaturated (imaginative) enough to encompass many possible contexts, thereby increasing the chances that one of them might correspond to reality and consequently stimulate illumination and growth in the mind of the patient.

In the course of an analysis, the analyst observes psycho-analytic elements – sensory representations imbued with emotion and embodying *ex hypothesi* a literal or non-literal truth. They are insights into the patient's world, and, however mysteriously, make some sense. But what sense? These elements connect in various ways to other elements, and their meaning consists precisely of the network that comprises the connections. This network constitutes the context in which these elements occur. For the psychoanalyst, these elements and the ways in which they are connected must be taken as givens, just as the physical scientist takes his sensory perceptions as givens: they are not to be agreed with or disputed, confirmed or discon-firmed, but only explored.

The analyst assumes that both analyst and patient are engaged in an attempt to define the patient's emotional experi-ences through careful observation, and, having observed them, to determine their meaning through further careful observations of the links that these experiences have with other emotional experiences.

Taking the patient's expression of emotional experience as a given that is not to be endorsed, disputed, proven or disproven, but simply regarded as fact, constitutes empathy in a uniquely psychoanalytic (and unsentimental) sense. The importance of such psychoanalytic empathy in Bion's view of the matter cannot be overemphasized. The analyst's first and most import-ant task is to observe as many facets of the patient's emotional experience as he can, in as much detail as he can. Bion writes:

> The more nearly he is able to approximate to this ideal, the nearer he is to the first essential in psycho-analysis – or, for that matter, any other science – namely, correct observation. The complement of the first essential is the last essential – correct interpretation. By "first" essential I mean not only priority in time but priority in importance, because if an analyst can observe cor-rectly there is always hope; it is of course a big "if". Without the last essential he is not an analyst, but if he has the first essential he may become one in time;

without it he can never become one, and no amount of
theoretical knowledge will save him.

[8, p. 14]

Having identified observation of the patient's emotional experiences as the foundation of psychoanalytic perception, Bion
addresses the second part of the analyst's work – determining
their meaning.

> This brings me to reconsideration of the nature of
> interpretation . . . if observation is sound, the conclu-
> sion that certain observed phenomena appear to
> approximate to a psychoanalytical theory will also be
> sound. But the soundness of the conclusion is impaired
> if the theory, which is always a preconception . . .
> colours the selection of the facts to be observed. The
> object [is to develop a preconception] in the analyst that
> is not directly psychoanalytical so that the observations
> made are not such that they are bound to approximate
> to a psychoanalytical theory. For if the preconception is
> psychoanalytical, there is clearly a risk that the obser-
> vations made under such a preconception appear to
> approximate to a psychoanalytical theory because they
> in fact derive from it. Such a condition amounts to
> circular argument.
>
> [8, p. 15]

Analysts must not have psychoanalytic theories in mind when
they observe the patient, because of the risk that such theories
will foreclose observation and lead analysts to "see" only what
conforms to what they brought to the session. (Of course, any
theory, psychoanalytic or not, poses this hazard to observation
of the patient.)

Since it is clear that no observation can be completely free
from premises (preconceptions), all observations would therefore seem to be doomed to circularity – doomed to return in the
end to the premises from which they started.

Bion acknowledges that there is no absolute way to avoid
circularity, so he turns his attention to considering how best to
live with it. He observes:

Experience of the circular argument, of which I have had a considerable amount, has convinced me that there is not much wrong with its logic, that it involves acceptance of a theory of causation, and that probably any logical argument is essentially circular. Since I am disposed to believe this of even classical instances of logical inquiry, I felt that the failure of circular arguments . . . to lead to any development had to be sought elsewhere than in their circularity.

[8, p. 18]

Bion is alluding here to the fact that a formal logical argument consists of showing that the proposition that is to be proven ("A is B") is logically equivalent to a tautology. In other words, a formal logical argument has the structure: "B is just a form of A, so when I say that A is B, I am really only saying that A is A, which is indisputably true". Despite this, many logical arguments are quite illuminating. Bion suggests that such illumination comes from the breadth of the argument's scope:

I decided that the difficulties that arose depended (to extend the use of the circle as a model) on the diameter. If the circular argument has a large enough diameter, its circular character is not detected and may, for all I know, contribute to useful discoveries.

[8, p. 18]

He goes on to illustrate the significance of this point for psychoanalysis with a clinical vignette concerning a psychotic patient who,

though aware of the approach of a car, walked out in front of it, was knocked down, and sustained minor injuries. This result was apparently quite unexpected. Many of his statements had prepared me to expect that he was dominated at the time of the event by the conviction that he was a puff of flatus [a fart].

[8, p. 16]

71

He then says that "the statements amounting to an assertion that he was a puff of flatus constitute an example of what I mean by theory" [8, p. 16].

Bion considered that the patient walked in front of the car not as an attempt to establish the empirical truth or falsity of his theory, like a scientist, but to discover its meaning, like a psychoanalyst. A patient's

> statement is never right or wrong but only meaningful. Any view that the episode was an empirical testing of a hypothesis leads to a dead end. But if it is regarded as a theory first intended to [define something], and thereby to take the first step in establishing the meaning of [what has been defined], certain aspects of the episode become clearer.
>
> [8, p. 16]

Asking what one's theory means is clearly different from, and clearly a prerequisite to, determining its empirical validity.[2]

There was nothing in the patient's view of himself – nothing that the patient could imagine – that would allow him in any serious way to consider that he was not a puff of flatus. Because of this, his view could not be linked to any context other than itself, and therefore no development – no investigation of what his theory meant – was possible.

The patient's problem was not simply that he was trapped in a circular argument, but was rather the fact that the "circle" of his argument did not exceed a point – its diameter was zero.

Bion told the patient that he had a fantasy that he was a puff of flatus. The patient was unable to understand this interpretation. Bion gives two reasons why: the first was that his use of the word "fantasy" in his interpretation caused the patient to think of psychic reality, which he was quite loath to do; the second was that the interpretation as a whole led the patient to

---

2 Compare this to Quine's proposal [31] that the unit of empirical significance in a field of investigation is the entire field of investigation. No theory is an island: a theory isolated from all other theories has no meaning and testing it produces results that cannot be interpreted.

feel that, if *only* a fantasy corresponded to his view of himself (which, we recall, he held as a conviction), others would think him mad.

Bion goes on:

> A week or ten days elapsed after the episode of the accident had been produced in analysis. The time was taken up with many interpretations, including attempts to draw his attention to the circular argument. I did not say it was of small diameter, but I had this in mind myself. I was also able to show him his fear of any interpretation that drew his attention to the fact that he had two dissimilar views about the same facts. The interpretations were not new but appeared to produce a response in him . . .
>
> Then, not having directly referred to the episode again after his first mention of it, he said the car driver had called him a fucking fool. I feel better now, he said. I took this to mean that his circular progress had brought him round to the point on the circle that was 'opposite' the statement that the car had collided with him. In time, at least, the argument was a circle of measurable diameter. But during that period of circular argument we had had opportunity for a number of interpretations, including the interpretation that he felt he was a puff of flatus. I therefore said that he felt the car accident was a sexual intercourse between a puff of flatus and the car and its driver. He said he felt better and added he felt he was going mad.
>
> The point I wish to illustrate is that the circular argument of small diameter though it precludes the matching or correlation of two statements and is therefore sterile, is preferred [by the patient] to the argument in a circle of relatively wide diameter because of the risk of a matching of two ideas that is accompanied by a feeling of madness. There is implicit in this the possibility that there must be distance between the correlated statements if meaning is to be achieved. If 'madness' is feared, the operation that leads to meaning is avoided. The circular argument must therefore be of small

diameter to prevent the conjunction of meaning and a
feeling of madness.

[8, pp. 19–20]

The driver's view of the patient (that he was "a fucking
fool"), when put together with the patient's view of himself (that
he was a puff of flatus), spanned a circle of some diameter.
What had happened was that the patient had allowed into his
mind something outside the compass of his "theory" about
himself, that is, something to which his theory could be linked,
against which it could be compared, and into the context of
which it might be set. This development provided little support
for the theory to which the patient was committed and led
immediately to the realization that his theory might require
some modification. The "madness" that he feared was a sense of
persecution associated with the ominous feeling that change
might be unavoidable.

When the patient said that the driver of the car had called
him "a fucking fool", Bion said that the collision represented
an intercourse between a puff of flatus and the car. The fact
that the patient could have this association itself meant that the
patient could entertain the driver's point of view, a view of the
patient from a vertex different from that of the patient, alongside his own. This resulted in an intercourse in the patient's
mind between his view of himself – that he was a puff of flatus
– and the driver's view of him – that he was a fool. This
juxtaposition of two distinct and distant views of the same
thing was an enlargement of the circle in which the patient's
view of himself traveled. This enlargement corresponds to a
psychoanalytic development, which carried with it as by-
products the simultaneous feelings that he was better (since he
recognized that he was able to allow some empirical observation to coexist with his theory of himself, and that he therefore had some potential for development) and that he was
going "mad". Here, "mad" refers to his sense that he had a
potential for development or change, just as "better" does. The
two are both experiences of the same thing from rather different
points of view.

The patient now could (at least momentarily) entertain a
perspective that moved him off the point to which he was

fixed and into a broader arc. This was a genuine development. It did not consist of the empirical verification or disconfirmation of the patient's theory, but of a matching of two different views of the same thing that illuminated the structure of his theory and its logic. It did not answer the question, "Is this theory true?", but it did give at least a partial answer to the question, "Assuming (by definition) that my theory is true in some way, in what way (or context) is it true?"[3]

The answer is "in the context of fantasy only, completely detached from any contact with internal or external reality that might differ from it"; in other words, in the context of a zero-diameter circle. This presents the patient with a dilemma. From the point of view of his desire to "know" things omnisciently (meaning having his ideas be not only correct, but also the only possible word on the subject), anything that differs from the patient's assumption (fantasy) about himself is madness. From the opposite point of view, one that seeks differing experiences of the same thing so that its meaning may be gleaned from juxtaposing them (what Bion refers to as "a sexual intercourse" and what we might also call the desire to learn as opposed to the desire to "know"), being stuck in the one-dimensional world of a point circle is madness. So from either perspective, the patient ends up feeling mad. The news that he is mad could not be very gratifying to the patient, but he felt better because knowing he's mad makes it at least possible for him to understand why, which must in itself provide relief, however bad the news that accompanies it.

It is quite characteristic of Bion to introduce a discussion of some difficulty facing a practicing psychoanalyst by bringing in material from a psychotic patient. It is as though he is saying: the problems we face when we try to do psychoanalysis are not very different from those of someone who is simply trying to remain sane. It is our own tendency toward insanity that presents us with the greatest difficulties in our work.

Bion has introduced this vignette not simply to give an interesting example of a thought disorder (although it is that),

3 This is equivalent to saying, "Given that it is a fact that I have this theory, what does this fact mean?"

but to illustrate how broadening the diameter of one's circular argument can illuminate the meaning of its premises. He is suggesting that when the psychoanalyst is doing psychoanalysis properly, he is doing the same as the patient in his example: he is exploring the meaning (if any) of his own psychoanalytic theories by introducing into them his observations of the patient in the session. This exploration expands the diameter of these theories' admittedly circular arguments. An interpretation based only on the analyst's theories does not expand them, and does not help the patient; the circle is too small. But to the degree that the analyst allows his theories to be brought together with observations that differ from them, he experiences a sense of insecurity. The patient in his example experienced this insecurity as a feeling of losing his mind. The analyst must be prepared to tolerate similar feelings in himself if he is to work properly.

The point here is that any "enlargement of the circle", any growth, any new perspective that forces us to modify what we think we already know, produces both relief (a sense of liberation from the constraints of a small mental and emotional circle) and terror (a sense of insecurity that, if tracked down into the deeper levels of the mind, is found to bleed into an unconscious feeling of losing one's mind). This two-pronged experience is reminiscent of Rilke: "beauty is nothing but the beginning of terror that we can only just barely still stand".[4]

Bion's ideas suggest that an interpretation does no more than illuminate the meaning of our premises; that the patient's theories, the analyst's theories, and perhaps all theories, are circular; and that it is the analyst's job to determine what circles they travel in. Welcome or not, this investigation enlarges the circle.

4 My translation of the German text [33, p. 150].

8

TERROR AND THE ARCHAIC SUPEREGO

The ability to perceive internal and external reality and to know the meaning of what one perceives requires a free imagination. But imagination is never completely free of interference.

Since imagination, along with perception and judgment, is a private mental experience, whatever interferes with it must arise most immediately from the internal world.[1] This inhibiting force has the power to control the mind and to stifle perception, imagination and judgment. When these faculties become too free – that is, when they cross certain boundaries – there is a part of the mind that strikes terror into one's heart. This part of the mind is the archaic superego.

A sense organ for the perception of psychic reality

The difference between an ordinary sensory stimulus and a traumatic one is only a matter of degree: a stimulus is traumatic if its intensity exceeds a certain threshold determined by the qualities of the receptor for that particular stimulus. For example, light of a certain intensity gives rise to a visual sensation when it strikes the retina, but light of a sufficiently great

---

1 Private mental functions, being private, are not subject to threats from the external world unless they are "published" by being converted into action. But we are discussing thinking itself, not action. It could be argued that thoughts are feared because they have led in the past to actions that were punished. But even in this case, the inhibition would have had to become internalized, and, insofar as it affects present-day thinking, must still arise internally.

energy will burn the retina and cause traumatic blindness. Similarly, a sharp object applied very gently to the skin gives rise to a neutral or even mildly pleasant sensation; applied with more energy, it may cause pain; applied with sufficiently great energy, it not only produces acute pain, but also traumatizes the skin by lacerating it.

The location of the line dividing stimuli that are tolerable (and thus potentially capable of giving rise to information) from those that are traumatic depends on the capacity of the organism's sensory apparatus to absorb energy without sustaining damage. Soft skin is more vulnerable to trauma than skin that has been toughened. There is an inverse relationship between immunity from trauma and sensitivity: calloused skin is more resistant to trauma, but it is also less sensitive.

Freud modeled his concept of psychological trauma directly on physical trauma. Just as traumatic physical events are those that violate the integrity of the body, traumatic psychological experiences are those that violate the integrity of the psyche. These experiences are so overwhelming (or their meaning is so powerful) that their significance cannot be absorbed. Such experiences not only fail to give rise to understanding or to convey information, but also damage or overload the apparatus that *might* understand them (in the same way that a too powerful signal sent to an electronic device will not convey information, but burn it out). Without outside intervention, these experiences are doomed to remain meaningless sources of dread.

Psychological trauma, like physical trauma, is a product of both the objective nature of the traumatic event and the individual's capacity to absorb stimulation; events that are traumatic for one individual may be merely exciting for another (consider the reactions of younger and older children to amusement park rides), and experiences that may be informative for one individual may be simply traumatic for another (a trained epidemiologist may be horrified but enlightened by observing the devastation caused by a deadly epidemic in all its gory detail, whereas an unsophisticated observer may simply be horrified or traumatized).

The psyche of an infant, like its skin, has a low threshold for disruption. Just as an infant's skin requires special care to guard against physical trauma, so its psyche requires special care to guard against psychic trauma. Adults normally recognize this fact in the way in which they instinctively comfort and reassure infants by holding them gently and speaking to them in soothing or buoyant tones.

A calm adult is much better able than a distressed one to calm a distressed infant. This commonplace observation leads to the conclusion that infants, although entirely lacking the capacity to interpret the semantic content of speech, have a capacity that is both innate and acute to sense an adult's state of mind and to tune themselves into it.

What to a sophisticated observer is simply the sense that one gains about another person's mental state is, for infants, with their lower threshold for disruption, an experience bordering on the traumatic; virtually all of their experiences border on the traumatic, and may quickly cross that border if not carefully regulated. Since infants cannot provide the needed regulation, they must rely on their mother's capacity to do so as a surrogate for their own.

It is no small irony that the mother is also the source of much of the overwhelming emotion that the infant needs her help to regulate. By gratifying her infant, she evokes powerful feelings of pleasure and comfort, and by frustrating the baby (as she inevitably must), she evokes powerful feelings of distress, pain and discomfort. Both kinds of feeling may be traumatic simply because their power is too much for the infant to manage. Infants' lives depends on their mothers' care, and they act as though they know that their very survival depends on how they stand with their mothers. The term "mother's care" encompasses more than dutiful attention to an infant's physical needs; it also includes how she cares for her infant in the psychological sense of the word. Her state of mind is both a source of traumatic stimuli for the infant and the means to relieve their traumatic effect.[2]

Having experienced their mother's capacity to manage its feelings, which means having experienced her state of mind as a

---

2 See Meltzer's concept of the mother as "La Belle Dame Sans Merci" [30] for a discussion of some of the consequences of this fact.

container for its otherwise traumatic experiences, and having learned through this that its mental survival depends on her state of mind, infants, still unable to manage their own experiences, devote themselves instead to the only avenue available to them: managing their mother's state of mind in order to secure the containment they need for their mental survival. There is, as Winnicott said, no such thing as an infant. An infant in isolation does not exist, and an infant isolated from its mother quickly ceases to exist. Infants act as though they know this.

Infants must manage their mother's state of mind, because they need her state of mind to manage their own, and they do so by recruiting her presence (how easy is it to ignore an infant's cries?). An adult must attend to the physical realities of food, warmth and shelter in order to survive. Infants depend entirely on their mothers not only for these material provisions, but also for the psychological sustenance provided by her capacity to transmute what would otherwise be meaningless traumas (meaningless because traumatic and traumatic because meaningless) into manageable and meaningful psychological experiences. Infants are therefore totally preoccupied with securing the presence on which their lives (mental as well as physical) depend – an effort the success of which ultimately depends on their mothers' love and affection for them. The availability of this love and affection is, of course, not the infant's to command, another fact that does not escape it.

The origin of the archaic superego

I will now describe a model of how infants experience the world, and how they attempt to make their experience bearable and therefore potentially comprehensible. This model is no more than an imaginative conjecture.

For reasons I have just outlined, the mother's state of mind (or more precisely – and this turns out to be a crucial distinction – the infant's perception of her state of mind) becomes the central focus of the infant's reality. It is the key factor in the infant's efforts to cope with all other realities, and managing the mother's state of mind becomes synonymous with survival. The infant's experience combines a sense of utter helplessness with a sense of utter dependence on a force that is at once ineffable and completely beyond its control. It is as though the infant's minute-to-minute survival depends entirely on the good will of a God whose every purpose is completely unfathomable. Faced with the Kafkaesque terror of this dilemma, the infant is forced into the belief that it is in control of its mother in order to save itself from being overwhelmed by fear of capricious and always imminent death.

The mechanism it employs is a terror-diminishing delusion that the mother is in some way subject to its will. This delusion is equivalent to the belief that its mother is a part of the infant and therefore under its control (projective identification). The relief and security that this belief confers is purchased at a price: when the infant identifies its mother with itself so as to control her, it ends up feeling that she has become installed in its mind as a controlling internal presence whose view of reality becomes the only view the infant can safely entertain (in the same way that the infant feels – and needs to feel – that its view of things must be imposed on the mother if it is to guarantee her presence). This internal presence is the archaic superego: a superego that usurps (or has had delegated to it) the infant's ego function of reality testing – a new part of the mind whose view of reality overrides that of the infant's own ego.

The terror the infant feels when confronted with external reality is reduced to manageable proportions by its belief that it now controls and possesses the mother within itself; but in exchange for this security the infant has acquired a terrifying internal presence: this God responds to our prayers only on condition that we respond to Hers – that we follow without question the strictures of Her desires for us. If we fail to do so, we are worse off than we were in the Godless universe from which we had just escaped.

This archaic internal God, vital for survival when the infant's ego is immature, becomes a threat to the infant's independent development – its development of a mind of its own – as its ego matures. Maturation thus involves a metamorphosis of one's relationship to one's mother: she must be gradually relinquished as a source of security, and the growing child, in its struggle for independence, must face the insecurity with which this loss has left it.

What I have just described is, as I said, no more than an imaginative conjecture. But it is a compelling one, because, while we cannot know directly what infants experience, older children and adults do, in their unconscious minds, experience the world in precisely the way I have described: they have the capacity to sense states of mind in other people, using the part of their minds that Freud called a "sense organ for the perception of psychical qualities". When this intimate contact with another mind produces experiences that are strange, new, powerful, moving and out of control, experiences that seem the most alive and immediate, and that answer the need for emotional connection with another human, the effect is beautiful and terrifying in more or less equal proportion.

Confronted with experience, torn between its beauty and its terror, and reaching the point we cannot endure, we unconsciously retreat to the security of an illusory but omnipotent parent who is in control of an otherwise terrifying world. This parent is the archaic superego, whose strictures on the operations of our minds reflect the strictures that our unconscious infantile selves place on the mind of the parent on whose constancy our very survival depends. We therefore become in our minds just as constant (and hence unfree and unimaginative) as we require her to be. To save our lives, we become good citizens of an Orwellian internal world from which we must struggle to free ourselves if we are to call our lives our own.

9

PSYCHOANALYSIS, THE INDIVIDUAL AND THE GROUP

As a consequence of the psychological realignments of latency and adolescence, adults no longer turn to their parents for a sense of security as they did when they were children. But the beauty and terror of the world remain, and, if adults are less helpless than infants to cope with it, they still cannot bear it entirely alone. Adolescent and adult peer groups foster their members' creativity by providing them with ways to explore the beauty of the world that are beyond the capability of individuals working in isolation. They also, when necessary, provide their members with refuge from the terrors of the world through what we might call group security relationships.

The security relationship of an adolescent and, to a lesser but still important degree, of an adult to his group, inherits many aspects of the infant's relationship to its parents. Adults seeking security and reassurance may merge with peer groups just as infants merge with their mothers, with similar results on the independence of imagination, perception and judgment. The psychological structure that results from merger with a group is an archaic superego that embodies the mores of the group.

In his book *Experiences in Groups* [3], W.R. Bion suggested that all groups engage in two forms of activity. The first he called Work activity, which emerges when the group is in contact with the realities of the problems it confronts. In the Work mode, the group fosters creative exploration of the problems that face it. In addition to the specifics of the task at hand, a group confronts limits imposed on it by the fact that it has a finite time in which to solve the problems that face it, that it cannot know precisely what these problems are, that its power to effect solutions to the problems is circumscribed, and that it faces real risks if it attempts any solutions. In other words, the working group behaves as though it were aware of Hippocrates' aphorism about the practice of medicine: "the art is long, life is short, opportunity fleeting, experiment treacherous, and judgment difficult". Awareness of these facts produces a sense of insecurity that the group must tolerate if it is to perform its work, since work requires above all realistic engagement with problems. The severity of the insecurity is directly proportional to the urgency of the work in which the group is engaged.

This sense of insecurity leads to a second form of group activity, which Bion called Basic Assumption activity. Unlike Work activity, which requires painstaking thought and is always accompanied by insecurity, Basic Assumption activity is automatic and unpremeditated, and is directed entirely toward eliminating the insecurity that the group's working confrontation with reality has caused. Basic Assumption activity inclines the group to act quite uncritically on ideas that, however little foundation they may have in reality, are nonetheless quite effective in diminishing the sense of insecurity resulting from the group's realistic engagement with its task. If Work activity is founded on contact with reality, Basic Assumption activity is founded on faith in the power of the group's fundamental beliefs (what Bion called its Basic Assumptions) to solve, certainly and without serious risk, whatever problems it faces. In Basic Assumption mode, group members are like overwhelmed infants, turning to the group's Basic Assumption activity for security just as the infant turns to its mother.

Bion divided Basic Assumption activity into three broad categories on the basis of the fundamental belief the activity seemed to embody. The first, which he called Dependent activity, appears to be founded on the belief in a benevolent and omnipotent God who will ensure not only the group's survival, but also the realization of its goals. When influenced by this mentality, the members of the group believe that the group will accomplish its goals as long as they maintain an unwavering faith in this God.

The second type of Basic Assumption activity, which Bion called Fight-Flight activity, is founded on the belief that there is no problem that cannot be solved by the threat or actual application of sufficient violence, or, failing that, by skilful evasion.

The third type of Basic Assumption activity, which he called Pairing activity, is founded on the belief that if the members of the group wait patiently, eventually two of them will produce a solution to the problems that face the group by giving birth to a Messiah.

A group can never commit itself fully to acting on its Basic Assumption beliefs, since a group that did nothing but await God's providence, prepare for war (or devise plans for evading conflict), or wait for the Messiah would quickly perish, and the group acts as though it is aware of these perils. Basic Assumption beliefs are therefore always accompanied by the admonitory feeling that they must never be put into action.

If no group, no matter how powerful its Basic Assumptions, can ever abandon a realistic appreciation of the problems that confront it, no group, no matter how realistic its outlook, is ever completely free of Basic Assumption activity. The group deals with its active Basic Assumption activity by forming what Bion called Specialized Work Groups, whose function it is to partly satisfy Basic Assumption impulses while at the same time keeping them from interfering too much with the Work activity of the group.

In society at large, the Specialized Work Group that addresses Dependent Basic Assumption mentality is the Church, which expresses and sustains a powerful faith in a benign and omnipotent God while at the same time admonishing its members to take individual responsibility for their lives ("God helps those who help themselves"). Fight-Flight mentality is addressed by the institution of the military, which constantly emphasizes the need for military preparedness while also constantly warning that war is so horrible it must be avoided at any cost. The Pairing mentality finds expression in utopianism, the feeling that if one just waits long enough, a new regime will sweep away all problems – always keeping in mind that the Messiah will appear only in the future, never as a present reality.

It is important to distinguish Basic Assumption activity from realistic activity that may resemble it. An appropriate concern for the safety of the group against outside dangers, and the realistic provision of self-defense, for example, are not a Fight-

Flight type Basic Assumption activity, any more than an optimistic attitude toward the future is the same as waiting for a Messiah, or reliance on the wisdom and benevolence of a leader whom experience has shown to have those qualities is the same as relying on the omnipotence of a deity.

All groups require Basic Assumption activity because a group's contact with reality regularly produces a sense of insecurity that would grow to paralyzing proportions if the contact were not limited in some way. Basic Assumption activity diminishes contact with reality until the level of insecurity becomes just bearable. Work that would otherwise be impossible can then be carried out to the degree that the remaining contact with reality permits. A group's Basic Assumption and Work activities mold and shape each other, and together they determine the group's character.

Psychoanalysis as a group activity

We may consider the psychoanalytic dyad as a Bionian group consisting of patient and analyst. Its Work function is to establish contact with psychic reality. The Basic Assumption function of analysis is directed toward channeling that contact in a direction that does not produce excessive terror, thereby keeping the analytic relationship secure enough to continue.

Although Basic Assumption activity arises spontaneously, automatically and without premeditation, it is not random; it is related to the Work activity of the group, in the sense that specific types of work activity stimulate specific anxieties, whose mitigation requires equally specific Basic Assumption activities. For example, because psychoanalysis requires that two people work in isolation from the larger society to which they belong, it is a powerful stimulant to fantasies that they are engaged in sex ("What do they *do* alone in that room all that time?"). The anxiety associated with this suspicion gives rise to a comforting pairing fantasy of nonsexual procreation leading to the production of a Messiah who will solve the problems besetting analyst and patient (or in other words, produce a cure). This fantasy produces the conscious belief that "the therapeutic relationship" itself, independent of any actual work that might be done in the analysis, will eventually produce a cure.

86

If Basic Assumption beliefs are to provide the psychoanalytic dyad with the security it needs, they must remain unexamined: the emotional comfort they provide will not survive a too-scrupulous examination of their validity. The psychoanalytic Work Group bears a uniquely unstable relationship to its own Basic Assumption activity, since one of the primary tasks of psychoanalysis is to bring the analytic dyad's Basic Assumption beliefs to light. An analysis is therefore constantly flirting with the release of anxieties that would render it unsustainable. But if it does not flirt with this danger, it will never reach its goal of psychological growth. Psychoanalysis doesn't work if it doesn't cause insecurity. Doing analysis is like walking: we pitch ourselves forward into an unstable position, and then at the last moment thrust a leg out so we don't fall. Our posture remains the same as before, but we're a step ahead.

Psychoanalysis and imagination

Basic Assumption activity protects itself from critical scrutiny by, among other things, undermining the imagination – the apparatus for imagining that these assumptions might not be the only possibilities. In Basic Assumption mode, the analyst and patient experience freely imagined conjectures about the nature of the problems they face, or about possible solutions, as sacrilegious, mad or destructive precisely to the degree that they freely deviate from the active Basic Assumption mentality. Ordinary skepticism, so essential to the psychoanalytic work of distinguishing fantasies about reality from reality, becomes in the Basic Assumption mode a dangerous and immoral attitude.

For example, under the sway of Basic Assumption mentality, imagining that God is not omnipotent or not on the group's side (doubting the complete benevolence or efficacy of analysis) feels indistinguishable from moral collapse; imagining that the group's capacity for violence might not solve the problems it faces (doubting that analysis can really stamp out neurosis) becomes indistinguishable from cowardice and weakness; and not believing in the coming of the Messiah (doubting that a "good therapeutic relationship" will produce the analysis we want) feels like an expression of the most extreme and destructive cynicism.

A working psychoanalysis rearms the imagination by opening up new conceptual possibilities, thereby allowing us to think about the previously unthinkable. The more analysis undermines Basic Assumption activity by thinking about it critically, the more it awakens the anxiety that Basic Assumption activities put to sleep. This constant tension between the need to think and the need for security is characteristic of a working psychoanalysis; its absence is strong evidence that the analysis has stopped working.

Broadening the imagination expands the universe of possibilities while at the same time contracting the degree of certainty one had when faced with only one possibility. This lack of certainty, if carried far enough and honestly enough, eventually produces a sense of danger and insecurity,[1] which leads to the resurgence of Basic Assumption activity and a collapse of mental space by exclusion and scotomization of anxiety-producing possibilities, with its concomitant impoverishment of imagination.[2]

The work of the psychoanalytic Work Group is observation, particularly observation of the activities of the psychoanalytic Basic Assumption Group. Such observation undermines the effectiveness of those assumptions, thereby risking the release of unbearable anxiety. Psychoanalytic observation tests the limits of one's ability to tolerate insecurity.

---

1 Pascal: "Je m'affrai les espaces infinies" (Infinite space terrifies me).
2 In this connection, Donald Meltzer once suggested (personal communication) that a sense of omnipotence is no more than a poverty of imagination.

10

PSYCHOANALYTIC WORK

Psychoanalysis and Basic Assumption activity

Psychoanalysis is an intimate activity in which two people, bound together by the psychological force of their common work, approach the mind from a unique perspective. In this chapter, I will try to describe that perspective.

Since psychoanalysis is a form of work, it is prone to the anxieties and insecurities that work engenders. The members of the psychoanalytic group of two therefore try to control these anxieties by engaging in Basic Assumption activity. But as I indicated in Chapter 9, the psychoanalytic dyad bears what may be a unique relationship to its own Basic Assumption activity: one of the primary tasks of psychoanalysis is to bring the dyad's Basic Assumption beliefs to light.

To the degree that an analysis sheds light on the operative Basic Assumption, it renders the assumption susceptible to critical thought. The anxieties driving the activity then become manifest and available to conscious experience. It is not too much of an exaggeration to say that this provides almost all that is necessary for the analysis to move forward (aside, of course, from the ability to tolerate the resulting anxiety).

It may help to understand how psychoanalysis works by noting that its approach is the precise opposite of the conventional psychiatric approach of symptom removal. Instead of trying to expel or destroy symptoms, it aims to integrate them into the patient's mind through the explication of their meaning. For psychoanalysis, psychological symptoms are a kind of strangulated truth, and rather than targeting them for elimination, it regards them as signs that something has disconnected a significant experience from the mass of other, non-symptomatic significant experiences. From the psychoanalytic point of view, a symptom is a distortion of experience brought about by this disconnection. The aim of psychoanalysis is to restore the broken connection, thereby converting the distorted, disconnected experience (the symptom) into an ordinary connected one.[1]

Symptoms will disappear in the course of an analysis, but not because psychoanalysis removes them directly, or even because it removes them indirectly. It does neither; instead it renders them irrelevant. In the course of a successful analysis, one may observe the patient losing interest in a symptom that preoccupied him at the beginning of the analysis, as he becomes more interested in what it points to. At this stage, the symptom is about to disappear, or rather, is about to be replaced by the ordinary thought or experience of which it was the strangulated expression.

The fundamental difference between the psychoanalytic goal of integration and the psychiatric goal of symptom-removal becomes clear when we consider that, since psychoanalysts regard symptoms as indicators of mental contents that have lost their connection to the rest of the mind, the goal of removing the symptom directly seems to analysts equivalent to destroying the evidence that would help a rescue party locate the survivors of a disaster. Even this analogy fails to convey the full extent of the damage that symptom-removal does from the analytic point of view: for psychoanalysis, the disaster in question is precisely the severing of connections in the mind, of which the symptom is an indispensable sign and link. Removing symptoms therefore compounds the injury that gave rise to the symptom in the first place, which, from the psychoanalytic point of view, is a second disaster.[2]

1 As Freud put it with just the right amount of rueful irony, psychoanalysis converts hysterical misery to ordinary human suffering [9] (Studies on Hysteria. *Standard Edition of the Complete Psychological Works of Sigmund Freud*, 2: 305, 1895).
2 Symptom-removal through pharmacology or behavioral therapy undoubtedly provides immediate relief from suffering. In addition, for many patients these approaches are the only practical ones. The point I wish to make is that these approaches may have long-term consequences that need to be taken seriously.

But here is a dilemma: the alternative to this second disaster – recognizing the original disaster and repairing it by reconnecting split-off parts of the mind – may require a dedication so extreme that it may seem to approach reckless disregard of consequences. Bion once suggested that we focus on the role of Tiresias in the Oedipus myth, and if we do so, the story becomes a cautionary tale against such ruthless pursuit of the truth.

When Oedipus, King of Thebes, learned from the Oracle that the plague that was devastating his city was the result of an offense against the gods, he swore to seek out the source of the offense. But the blind seer Tiresias warned him that in doing so he was committing hubris and endangering himself. Despite this, Oedipus pressed on relentlessly until he identified the offense, but only at the cost of revealing a truth so unacceptable that it precipitated his ostracism from Thebes, his mother's suicide and his self-mutilation. This terrible misfortune seemed to validate Tiresias' warning that by undertaking his investigations, Oedipus was committing an act of hubris.

While we can acknowledge the psychological realism of this myth – the mind behaves *as if* a search for truth would bring on the dire consequences Oedipus suffered in the myth – it is important to note that the course of action the story warned us against is precisely the one that, from the psychoanalytic point of view, we need to relieve neurotic disability. We tolerate the plague of our neurotic symptoms because we fear that discovering the truths they simultaneously rest on and cover over will lead to our destruction. For the blinded patient, as for the blind Tiresias, they are a way of avoiding disaster; but for the psychoanalyst, severed connections in the mind *are* the disaster.

The patient's fear of discovering the truth is not entirely irrational, however. Unless something intervenes to prevent it, the patient *will* be destroyed by what he discovers; his archaic superego, ever intolerant of human nature, will ostracize and blind him. What psychoanalysis adds to the discussion is the observation that what the myth portrays as the natural law of hubris and nemesis is in fact an artifact produced by the archaic superego, which threatens to destroy us for being human.

(The Oedipus myth has a counterpart in the myth of the Garden of Eden, where Jehovah plays the role of Tiresias, warning that partaking of the fruit of the tree of knowledge will

91

lead only to destruction. While it is true that Adam and Eve's disobedience does bring death into the world, it also brings sexual creativity – in other words, life. By disobeying Jehovah's prohibition, the couple escaped a state that was neither alive nor dead.)

Because the archaic superego is such a destructive psychological force, we can sympathize with Tiresias' dread of discovering the truth: Oedipus discovered that he had been violating powerful taboos, injunctions against desires, actions, and ideas so dangerous that even thinking about them subjects the owner to destruction by the Basic Assumption Group (whose motto might be tranquility at all cost), or its intrapsychic representative, the archaic superego. Only by killing these ideas – disconnecting them from the main part of one's mind – and then covering up the disconnection (by a kind of self-mutilation of one's consciousness), can one save oneself from being identified with them and thereby becoming the target of the mob-like superego and the superego-like mob.

In the end, Oedipus, having wandered the earth in disgrace for years, finally came to understand his humanity and to achieve some shelter from the depredations of his superego. At home at last among the citizens of Colonus, whose pity for him some regard as a Sophoclean anticipation of Christian charity, he died peacefully in a state of grace that was denied to those who spurned and scorned him. He had achieved what is rare among men and even rarer among the powerful: he was an honest man.

Psychoanalytic integrity

"Worüber man nicht sprechen kann, darüber muss man schweigen." (Whereof one cannot speak, thereof must one remain silent) [37, p. 89]. With this aphorism, Wittgenstein expressed his respect for truth by admonishing us not to pretend we can know or express what we can't know or express: if you don't know what you're talking about, don't say anything. This essential advice applies to anyone who is trying to speak with integrity, who does not wish to misrepresent what he is speaking of, and who does not wish to misrepresent himself by creating the impression that he knows something he doesn't.

Psychoanalysts constantly violate this admonition. Because a psychoanalyst cannot *know* the experience of another person, any interpretation the analyst makes inevitably misrepresents that experience to some degree. Edward Glover's paper, "The therapeutic effect of inexact interpretation: A contribution to the theory of suggestion" [25], deals with the dangers of an analyst giving an interpretation that, while not perfectly accurate, comes close enough to be used as a plausible diversion from the truth. Glover is making an important point, but he does so by setting up a dichotomy between exact and inexact interpretations that is not precisely true: *all* interpretations are inexact, that is, less than perfectly full and accurate. Since the analyst cannot be omniscient, interpretations are only more or less inexact. But because the patient is always searching for the security that comes from certainty, an interpretation that is close enough to the truth poses the danger that the patient will give up his critical faculties and swallow it whole.[3] This inescapable damage is a consequence of the fact that Basic Assumption activity, in the form of the desire for secure knowledge operating at the expense of truth, always outruns the insight one might have into its manifold operations.

The analyst is like a surgeon cutting the body. However benign the analyst's intentions, and however good the overall result, it's no use pretending the analyst is doing no damage. In fact, it's worse than useless to pretend: the analysis itself must, among other things, attempt to repair the damage it is continually doing to the patient. This damage is an integral part of psychoanalysis, and must be recognized if the analysis is to retain its integrity.

The intimate psychological contact of an analysis, no matter how good and beneficial on the whole, is also still somehow a violation in the sense that Wittgenstein warned against ("Whereof one cannot speak, thereof must one remain silent"). The analyst's attempt to make contact with the patient is inevitably flawed and (to the degree that the patient accepts it

---

3 This is the danger that Glover [25] was warning us against. The fact that the patient may be a willing accomplice does not relieve the analyst of responsibility for his role in the matter.

uncritically) damaging. An interpretation always poses a danger to the patient, since it is always potentially wrong. This is, of course, no reason to abandon the search for truth. The danger consists not in the analyst's search for truth, and not even in the fact that his interpretations are inevitably flawed, but in his *not recognizing* that this is so; not in his making an attempt to say something previously unknown to the patient that touches him deeply, but in *not acknowledging* that his attempts to do so are inescapably flawed and cannot do justice to their subject. The damage occurs when the analyst and patient feel that interpretations may be uttered without doing damage.[4]

This damage is not the result of clumsy analysis; it is the result of skilful analysis. To the degree that analysts *do* know what they are talking about, their words penetrate the patient to produce powerful feelings of love (because the patient feels understood by the analyst) and dread (because the patient fears that the analyst will *mis*use this understanding to *mis*understand the patient the next time). This dread is not without reason.

Analysts cannot avoid damaging their patients. But if analysts are aware of the violence that the intimate relationship of psychoanalysis may do to a patient's mind, and of the need to safeguard and police their patients' capacity to think for themselves even under the difficult and challenging circumstance of being in analysis, analysts will be in a position to damage their patients responsibly.

Analysts need to have an attitude of skepticism and humility about their own observations, and to recognize that no interpretation is so accurate that the patient may accept it uncritically. This attitude will save analysts from analytic hubris, and at the same time create a setting that acknowledges destructiveness, including the destructiveness of psychoanalysis, as an inevitable part of living and creativity.

This setting provides a haven from persecution like that offered to Oedipus by the citizens of Colonus: permeated by a sense of sadness, awe and human limitations – and free of mindless violence.

---

4 Oedipus thought he could rid his city of the plague without damaging anything valuable. In my reading of the myth, this was his real hubris.

The theme of violence and shelter in Sophocles' *Oedipus* finds a parallel in another ancient Greek dramatic cycle, the *Oresteia* of Aeschylus: Orestes is pursued by the Erinyes, bizarre half-woman, half-bird creatures who persecute him for murdering his mother, Clytemnestra, and her lover, Aegisthus.[5] Orestes had killed them to avenge their murder of Orestes' father, Agamemnon. Clytemnestra had conspired with Aegisthus to murder Agamemnon because he had sacrificed his (and her) daughter, Iphigenia, to appease Poseidon. All of these calamities were manifestations of a curse placed on Agamemnon's father, Atreus, by Atreus' brother after Atreus had murdered and roasted his brother's children and, in the guise of hospitality, served them to his brother at a feast.

After many years of persecution by the Erinyes, Orestes finally flees to Athens, where the goddess Athena puts an end to the cycle of murderous retribution by giving shelter to Orestes and establishing the rule of law, thereby converting the Erinyes into benign guardians of the household (the Eumenides).

By recognizing and integrating the inevitability of human destructiveness, psychoanalysis, like the citizens of Colonus and the goddess Athena, puts an end to the cycle of violence and retribution presided over by the archaic superego. It protects patients from their mob-like, persecuting superego – the aspect of themselves that wants to murder them, blind them and drive them mad for being human.

Psychoanalysis works not only by being compassionate about human passions, like the citizens of Colonus, but also by being *dis*passionate about them as well, like Athena, the goddess of wisdom. A habit of mind that places a high value on truth, dispassionate observation and critical thought creates a setting that curbs violence.[6] A relentless commitment to evidence protects patients from being driven mad by their archaic superego. Like Athena, psychoanalysis makes responsibility bearable by

---

5 The Greeks believed that the Erinyes operated on their victims by disturbing the mind with unbearable feelings of persecution, leading to madness. The archaic superego works in the same way.

6 This habit of mind is part of the psychoanalytic perspective that I referred to in the opening paragraph of this chapter.

offering an orderly alternative to murderous retribution: it slowly converts the Erinyes-like, persecuting archaic superego into a mature superego, a kindly guardian of the internal household, a superego with a human face.

While the archaic superego deals in moral absolutes and certain knowledge (like religious fundamentalists, whose activities make them an external or social version of the archaic superego), psychoanalysis is concerned with reality and the limitations of knowledge. It recognizes that reality is what it is, and remains so quite independent of our opinions, which are no more than imperfect reflections of it.

The pretension to know in an absolute sense – to lose sight of the fact that our knowledge about anything is always incomplete – is connected to our need to escape the pain and terror of recognizing how vast the gulf is between our minds and the rest of the world. Our need to know more than we can, so we can feel we have more control than we do over the world beyond us on which our very survival depends, drives us to the delusion of knowing absolutely.

By supporting the patient's efforts to escape this kind of absolutism and to tolerate the terror and insecurity of facing an uncontrollable reality, analysis helps the patient's ego gain ascendance over its archaic superego and transform it into a mature superego – a transformation of moralism based on omniscience and the delusion of control into morality based on truth and the awareness of limits.

Psychoanalysis and truth

In his book *Transformations* [6, pp. 37–8], Bion attempts to explore the relationship of psychoanalysis to truth by delineating the difference between propaganda and the explorations that lead to truth. He begins by pointing out that what the analyst does with the patient's communications can be divided into two broad categories, depending on the analyst's intent.

The first category consists of the analyst's verbalizations of his experiences in the session. This kind of interpretation is not a claim to know what is in the patient's mind, but merely an attempt by the analyst to convey his own experience – to give their own take (acknowledged as such) on what the patient is communicating – in order to demonstrate something to the patient with the implication that the analyst feels it is something worth considering, without the implication that it must be true, and with no eye to how the patient might respond to it emotionally. When the analyst is doing this, according to Bion,

> the analyst's position is akin to that of the painter who by his art adds to the public's experience. Since psychoanalysis does not aim to run the patient's life but to enable him to run it according to his lights and therefore to know what his lights are, [the analyst's interpretation] should represent the psychoanalyst's verbal representation of an emotional experience . . . [This] verbal expression must be limited so that it expresses truth without any implication other than the implication that it is true in the *analyst's opinion*.
>
> [6, p. 37, original emphasis]

Analysts must make clear that they are only rendering an opinion, thereby undermining the patient's idealizations of their words as revealed or absolute truth, an idealization that places analysts in the position of an archaic superego, and that not only relieves the patient of the need to think any further, but also inhibits the patient from doing so even if he wants to.

The second category consists of interpretations that attempt to induce a calculated emotional state in the patient for "therapeutic" reasons. Bion describes this as

> repugnant to psychoanalytic theory and practice. The painter who works on the public's emotions with an end in view is a propagandist with the outlook of a poster artist. He does not intend his public to be free in its choice of the use to which it puts the communication he makes.
>
> [6, p. 37]

Bion feels that distinguishing between tendentiously manipulating the patient's emotions (i.e., propagandizing the patient) on the one hand, and something like artistic or scientific integrity on the other – is valuable because analysts need to make this distinction if they are to preserve the integrity of their work. But, he goes on to ask, what does integrity mean in psychoanalysis?

> How is truth to be a criterion . . . To what has it to be true and how shall we decide whether it is or not . . . Falling back on analytic experience for a clue . . . the problem arises with schizoid personalities in whom the superego appears to be developmentally prior to the ego and to deny development and existence itself to the ego. The usurpation by the superego of the position that should be occupied by the ego involves imperfect development of the reality principle, exaltation of a "moral" outlook and lack of respect for the truth. The result is starvation of the psyche and stunted growth. I shall regard this statement as an axiom that resolves more difficulties than it creates.
>
> [6, pp. 37–8]

Bion's axiom implies that the search for truth is as vital to the mind as the search for food is to the organism. Anything that seriously threatens the search for truth threatens the life of the mind.

When Pilate asked, "What is truth?", Jesus replied that it was the man who stood before him. Bion answers, in effect, "observations made from a state of mind in which ego function is not usurped by the superego", a drier and less poetic response than the more famous one, perhaps, but good enough for our purposes.

The archaic superego – the superego that usurps ego function – replaces learning from experience with a "moral" outlook that is well expressed by the mutilation of Oedipus and the persecution of Orestes by the Erinyes. The point, of course, is not that there's nothing wrong with incest or matricide. It's that the punishment of these two men (one's crime based on ignorance, and the other's on the desire to avenge the murder of his father) is so relentless, destructive and intense that it becomes a criminal act in itself. A superego such as this presides over a fundamentalist regime in which free inquiry is an enemy of the state (as Oedipus' father Laius regarded the infant Oedipus), to be murdered at birth (as Oedipus would have been had his father's plan not miscarried). Such severity renders impossible the free, imaginative inquiry that the personality needs if it is to observe, think, and discover the truth that sustains it.

Creativity is disciplined by observation, and a true creation (artistic or scientific) conveys an observation of some truth purely for the sake of conveying it, not for the sake of using it as propaganda. Observation depends in turn on the creative freedom to see things as they are.

Creativity resides in the part of the personality in which the beauty of the world combines with the courage to engage it, emboldening the ego to create for itself. The intrapsychic exemplar of beauty lies in the child's apprehension of its beautiful mother, beautiful because she is the source of its life as well as of the psychological containment that helps the child bear the terror of her beauty. The intrapsychic exemplar of courage is the child's appreciation of its father – courageous because, despite his own fears, he risks his safety to shelter and defends her against the dangers that would damage or destroy her.[7]

The development of children's creativity depends on their allowing these mysterious parental qualities to combine in a spontaneous creative intercourse. When the beauty of truth (which is also terrifying) combines with the courage to defend it from assaults, the result is creativity. While the archaic superego usurps ego function and destroys creativity, the mature superego fosters ego function and is the source of creativity. The mature superego is the product of the child's successful Oedipal struggle to allow his parents to combine spontaneously and mysteriously – that is, beyond his control and in ways that surpass his understanding. If the child has resolved his Oedipal conflict in a healthy way by accepting the gulf between himself and his parents (which is another way of saying that he has accepted his position in the Oedipal triangle), he can allow the parents to possess the qualities of beauty and courage and to

---

7 I call these presences *intrapsychic* exemplars because they exist in the mind. Their relationship to the external parents is a complex one. They are models or ideals, and what is important is for the child to have in its mind the concept of such beauty and courage as something to which it may aspire, regardless of the degree to which the actual parents embody these qualities or fail to do so.

combine them together in their creative union. He will consequently possess a mature superego that not only allows him to create for himself, but also provides a muse-like source of creative inspiration.

We become free to create only to the degree that we overcome our need, driven by fear and insecurity, to imprison these vital parental presences inside ourselves. Such imprisonment stifles them and deprives them of their own free creativity, leaving us able only to mimic their smothered existence. By freeing them, and paying a price in the resultant insecurity, we can live under their aegis, respected by them as we respect them, free to know and to create for ourselves what is real.

REFERENCES

[1] Cyril Barrett. *Lectures and Conversations on Aesthetics, Psychology and Religious Beliefs*. University of California Press, Berkeley, CA, 1966.

[2] Bruno Bettelheim. *Freud and Man's Soul*. Knopf, New York, 1983.

[3] Wilfred R. Bion. *Experiences in Groups, and Other Papers*. Basic Books, New York, 1961.

[4] Wilfred R. Bion. *Learning from Experience*. Heinemann, London, 1962. Also in *Seven Servants*. Jason Aronson, New York, 1977.

[5] Wilfred R. Bion. *Elements of Psychoanalysis*. Heinemann, London, 1963. Also in *Seven Servants*. Jason Aronson, New York, 1977.

[6] Wilfred R. Bion. *Transformations*. Heinemann, London, 1965. Also in *Seven Servants*. Jason Aronson, New York, 1977.

[7] Wilfred R. Bion. *Clinical Seminars and Four Papers*. Fleetwood Press, Abingdon, UK, 1987.

[8] Wilfred R. Bion. *Taming Wild Thoughts*. Karnac, London, 1997.

[9] Joseph Breuer and Sigmund Freud. Studies on Hysteria. *Standard Edition of the Complete Psychological Works of Sigmund Freud*, 2, 1895.

[10] Robert Caper. Does psychoanalysis heal? A contribution to the theory of psychoanalytic technique. *International Journal of Psycho-Analysis*, 73: 283–92, 1992. Reprinted in *A Mind of One's Own*, Routledge, London, 1999, pp. 19–31.

[11] Robert Caper. What is a clinical fact? *International Journal of Psycho-Analysis*, 75(5/6): 903–13, 1994. Reprinted in *A Mind of One's Own*, Routledge, London, 1999, pp. 45–58.

[12] Robert Caper. Squaring the circle: A review of *Taming Wild Thoughts* by W.R. Bion. *Psychoanalytic Books*, 10(2): 125–133, 1999.

[13] Robert Caper. *Immaterial Facts: Freud's Discovery of Psychic Reality and Klein's Development of his Work*. Routledge, London, 2000.

[14] Robert Caper. The goals of clinical psychoanalysis: Notes on interpretation and psychological development. *Psychoanalytic Quarterly*, 70(1): 99–116, 2001.

[15] Freeman Dyson. *The Scientist as Rebel*. New York Review Books, New York, 2006.

[16] Ernst L. Freud, editor. *Letters of Sigmund Freud, 1879–1939*. Hogarth, London, 1961.

[17] Sigmund Freud. Charcot. *Standard Edition of the Complete Psychological Works of Sigmund Freud*, 3: 11–23, 1893.

[18] Sigmund Freud. Psychical (or mental) treatment. *Standard Edition of the Complete Psychological Works of Sigmund Freud*, 7: 283–302, 1905.

[19] Sigmund Freud. Psychische behandlung (seelenbehandlung). *Gesammelte Werke, Chronologisch Geordnet*. S. Fischer Verlag, Germany, 1905.

[20] Sigmund Freud. Recommendations to physicians practising psychoanalysis. *Standard Edition of the Complete Psychological Works of Sigmund Freud*, 12: 111–20, 1912.

[21] Sigmund Freud. Introductory Lectures on Psychoanalysis. *Standard Edition of the Complete Psychological Works of Sigmund Freud*, 15–16, 1915–17.

[22] Sigmund Freud. Two encyclopedia articles. *Standard Edition of the Complete Psychological Works of Sigmund Freud*, 18: 235–259, 1923.

[23] Sigmund Freud. Postscript to "the question of lay analysis". *Standard Edition of the Complete Psychological Works of Sigmund Freud*, 20: 251–8, 1927.

[24] Sigmund Freud. An outline of psycho-analysis. *Standard Edition of the Complete Psychological Works of Sigmund Freud*, 23: 144–267, 1940.

[25] Edward Glover. The therapeutic effect of inexact interpretation: A contribution to the theory of suggestion. *International Journal of Psycho-Analysis*, 12: 397–411, 1931.

[26] Michel Gribinski. The stranger in the house. *International Journal of Psycho-Analysis*, 75: 1011–21, 1994.

[27] Ilse Grubrich-Simitis. *A Phylogenetic Fantasy: Overview of the Transference Neuroses*. Harvard University Press, Cambridge, MA, 1987.

[28] Ernest Jones. *The Life and Work of Sigmund Freud*. Basic Books, New York, 1953.

[29] Ernst Kris. Review of "Freudianism and the Literary Mind" by Frederick J. Hoffman (published Baton Rouge: Louisiana State

University Press, 1945). *Psychoanalytic Quarterly*, 15: 226–34, 1946.

[30] Donald Meltzer and Meg Harris Williams. *The Apprehension of Beauty: The Role of Aesthetic Conflict in Development, Art and Violence*. Clunie Press, Old Ballechin, Strath Tay, Scotland, 1988.

[31] Willard van Orman Quine. Two dogmas of empiricism. In *From a Logical Point of View*, pp. 20–46. Harper and Row, New York, 1961.

[32] John Rickman. Methodology and research in psychopathology. In *Selected Contributions to Psycho-Analysis*. Hogarth Press and the Institute of Psycho-Analysis, London, 1957. First published in *British Journal of Medical Psychology*, 24(1): 1–7, 1951.

[33] Rainer Maria Rilke. *The Selected Poetry of Rainer Maria Rilke*. Edited and translated by Stephen Mitchell. Vintage International, New York, 1989.

[34] Tim Rutten. Spirit of Beckett guides the week. *Los Angeles Times*, October 15, 2005.

[35] F.E. Schlossman. Frage des hospitalismus im sauglingsaustalten. *Zeitschrift fur Kinderheilkunde*, 1926.

[36] Giovanni Vassalli. The birth of psychoanalysis from the spirit of technique. *International Journal of Psycho-Analysis*, 82: 3–25, 2001.

[37] Ludwig Wittgenstein. *Tractatus Logico Philosophicus*. Routledge, London, 2001.

INDEX

Note: Entries marked with a page number followed by an 'n' refer to the relevant Footnote on that page.

superego *see* archaic superego;
  mature superego
surprise 12

techne 47–8, 49
telepathy 25
terror 56, 57, 76, 80–2
thinking and feeling 60
truth 14, 15, 55–6, 91, 96–100

unconscious 10, 11, 20, 22, 41–2,
  45, 59–60

Valéry, Paul 62
Vassalli, Giovanni 42, 44–5, 46, 47

Wittgenstein, Ludwig 23, 92, 93
Work activity 83–4